The Allyn and Bacon Guide
to Writing Portfolios

Gina Claywell
Murray State University

Allyn and Bacon
Boston · London · Toronto · Sydney · Tokyo · Singapore

Table of Contents

Preface

When I first signed the contract to write this book, my eight-year-old son, Charlton, excitedly gave me some wise advice: "Mom," he said, "make it big, make it exciting, and use lots of examples." The book was never planned to be big in size, but I do hope students find it to be both exciting and big on ideas that will help improve portfolio writing. To satisfy students and my son alike, examples are included from my former students who have so graciously agreed to let me use their work.

The premise operating herein is that the advice in this text may seem apparent to instructors but rarely so to students. I frequently hear the admonitions from this book spoken at conferences, in teaching methods courses, and among my peers in the hallways: "If only my students would choose better pieces to put in their portfolio" or "I can read the revision statement and tell a whole lot about the portfolio." Somehow, though, we never think to tell students in any methodical way all the tips that can help them fashion a portfolio that they can be proud to submit and that we are pleased to read. So, this text offers students just such no-longer-confidential advice.

In writing the book, I am again reminded of how indebted I am to all of my former students who have probably taught me much more than I have ever imparted to them. To that same effect, I want to thank my former colleagues at East Central University for teaching me what an English professor is, does, and can be. For that same reason, I am also grateful to the English Department faculty at Murray State University; thanks especially to Dean Ken Wolf and Department Chair Peter Murphy for both the course release and for being so understanding of my need to devote attention to this text. This text would not have developed without the prompting of Allyn & Bacon representative Mark Apple, the encouragement of Eben Ludlow, and the organization of Grace Trudo. I am also indebted to the excellent recommendations from the proposal and first-draft reviewers, to Faye Smith (mom!) for her assistance in editing, and Heath Keller of the MSU ACTS office for help with scanning the student portfolios.

Finally, I want to thank Charlton, his sister Catherine, and their father Gerald for making life so intensely rewarding and for being so understanding when I am, quite simply, a grouch. This text is dedicated to them.

gsc 5/19/00

Chapter 1
Determine What is Expected of You

*"Learning occurs best if learners understand early
what is to be learned and how it is to be learned"
(Sheckley and Keeton 5).*

Can you answer the following?

➢ How will your portfolio be used?

➢ What type of portfolio are you preparing?

➢ What is the goal of your portfolio?

➢ Who is the audience for your portfolio?

➢ What is the role of that audience?

This chapter will help you find the answers.

Portfolio usage is increasing in college and university classrooms regardless of discipline: "Portfolios are scarcely a new concept, but renewed interest . . .has recently increased their visibility and use" (Arter, Spandel, and Culham 1). Instructors who read portfolios as a regular part of their duties, however, often find that student writers do not always understand the exact purpose of the portfolio, what should be in it, or how it should be presented. In fact, portfolio researchers admit, "There is no easy formula for writing a good portfolio..." (Decker, Cooper, and Harrington 98). Another researcher suggests, ". . .no consensus exists as to how portfolios should look, what they should contain, how they should be read, or who should assess them" (Callahan 118). Since so much disparity exists between what students submit and what teachers expect, it makes sense that the first step to compiling your portfolio should be understanding what portfolios are.

You may not be sure what some of the terms associated with a portfolio mean, or you may fear the negative impact on your course grade that might result from a poorly constructed portfolio. Even the strongest of writers may experience apprehension. Such concern was made clear (and led to the development of this book) when a Senior English major with strong writing skills attached a note to her portfolio reflection statement which stated that she had no idea what the statement should look like, sound like, or include. If submitting a portfolio is in your near future, you may feel similarly clueless.

This text is designed to help you create the best possible portfolio you can. After all, as educator Marianne Tully points out, "The greatest evidence of a student's growth as a writer can be found in a well-constructed portfolio consisting of carefully selected examples of that student's writing" (90). Since portfolios generally have deadlines and time is passing, let's begin work on your portfolio right now by deciphering some of the language surrounding portfolios. (A glossary is provided as Appendix A for future reference.) This chapter will help you understand what type of portfolio you need to submit, what the portfolio's goals are, and for whom you're writing the portfolio.

Uses of Portfolios

Portfolios are useful assessment tools for student writing. Portfolio researchers at Eckerd College in St. Petersburg, Florida, have found that, with portfolios,

> Students are invited to extend their view of writing beyond the closure of 'term papers' and the artificial boundaries of semesters, to see writing as involving recursive processes of critical thinking, expressing, rethinking, and revision. (Harrison 44)

In a college or university setting, portfolios generally fall into the categories of Individual Course Portfolios, Program Assessment Portfolios, or Student Career Portfolios. Let's explore the difference and the impact of these portfolios on both students and programs, because knowing more about these portfolios can affect how you undertake the task of compiling a portfolio.

Individual Course Portfolios

The Individual Course Portfolio reflects the work of a course in a given semester or quarter. Such portfolios generally do not extend beyond the length of the course unless the instructor keeps the portfolio for a specified amount of time before returning the portfolio; this happens often for several reasons: in the event of a grade appeal, to provide actual student writing for the instructor's research, and to provide teaching evidence for the instructor's portfolio.

Individual Course Portfolios exist in a variety of disciplines, and research indicates that they are becoming increasingly more popular at least in part because they help instructors more accurately assess student ability:

> Those who are most comfortable with grading student writing see portfolios as a way to ensure that the grades they must assign at the end of the semester are as fair as possible. For these teachers, portfolios are attractive because they allow a more accurate assessment of what a student is able to do at the end of the course than is a traditional average based on a set of individual attempts at each assignment. (Callahan 122)

These Individual Course Portfolios usually "…belong more to the student. . .treat student self-reflection as essential for learning. . .and require more time and skills for students to manage" (Arter, Spandel, and Culham 3).

The wide variety of portfolios that exist—from math to writing to the more traditional portfolio fields of art and photography—would suggest that their finished products might vary considerably, which they do. However, with the exception of portfolios that focus on visuals more than on the written word, such as art and photography, many constants exist concerning what should be included in a portfolio across any discipline. The specific features of such portfolios, including the amount and types of material to include, will be addressed throughout this text—and especially in Chapter 4—and there are, moreover, consistent rewards for compiling a portfolio in any courses you might take.

The greatest incentive you may have for completing a portfolio remains the impact such assignments have on your course grade. However, just as the requirements for portfolios in various courses vary, so do the percentages which portfolios are worth. A wide range exists between how significant portfolios are in any given course—indeed the same course requiring portfolios might vary from instructor to instructor in the weight assigned to portfolios. For instance, Murray State University professor Sue Sroda devotes 20% of the course grade to portfolios in her upper-level technical writing course. Instructor Lisa Wilson also allots 20% of the course grade in her first-year composition courses to portfolios. My own writing intensive courses likewise devote one-fourth of the course grade to portfolios. At Purdue's Developmental Writing Program, however, the portfolio is worth about 70% of the grade (Weiser 90).

The most crucial factor is that you realize the portfolios' relative worth as you compile it. If the portfolio comprises a large percentage of the course grade, you will, of course, want to devote a significant amount of time to the portfolio. Find out the portfolio percentage by closely examining the course syllabus or, if that is not clear, by asking your instructor.

Program Assessment Portfolios

Another broad category of portfolios involves a college or university's assessment of its programs and/or its faculty's effectiveness. Usually, such a portfolio—often called a portfolio test, proficiency portfolio, or accountability portfolio—is collected at the end of a program of study. For example, some schools require all sophomores to submit a portfolio following completion of general education requirements. Many universities offering teaching certificates require portfolios from all of their education majors. (See Appendix B for specific information about Teacher Education portfolios). Often, departments such as English ask all majors to submit portfolios during their senior year. The use of such portfolios overall is growing as Callahan notes: "…the growing popularity of portfolio tests is an important educational trend at all levels of American education" (126). The Program Assessment Portfolios are usually "more structured …belong to the institution…and require more time and skills for teachers to manage" (Arter, Spandel, and Culham 3). These and similar portfolios may potentially affect both you and the programs at your university or college.

Student Career Portfolios

Similar to a program assessment portfolio, the Student Career Portfolio tracks the progress you make as a student throughout a program or during your entire stay at a college or university. Its main difference is in its focus on encouraging you to assess your personal growth more than on assessing the university's role. Often, a Student Career Portfolio will be useful for securing employment after graduation; this works best, of course, when the portfolio is related to your major. Such portfolios have been called "passportfolios," "certificates of competence," or "employment skills portfolio" and show students' "readiness to move on to a new level of work or employment" (Arter, Spandel, and Culham 2; Lankes 2). However, even if the material does not serve as evidence to future employers, portfolios can give you positive reminders of the knowledge you gained and of your successful mastery of a subject.

Effects on Students

Any of the portfolio types can impact either your course grade or your ability to enter a program of study or even your ability to graduate. Especially if you are taking a "Capstone" course—the last course of your general education requirements or of your major program—you will want to read the portfolio requirements carefully. Check to see whether or not your successful completion of the portfolio will affect your grade or your ability to advance in your academic career. Although knowing this will help you know the relative amount of time you should devote to the presentation of your portfolio, you will, naturally, want to do your best in either scenario. An added incentive is that what appears to be a highly successful portfolio might give instructors an additional reason for recommending you for future course- or work-related opportunities. Because portfolios capture a "moment in time" by portraying your best work at the end of a course or program, they often serve other purposes such as providing samples of your work to potential employers.

Also, Program Assessment Portfolios can possibly impact the teacher-student relationship by encouraging you and your instructor to work together to prepare your portfolio for judgment by outside critics. Callahan likens this possibility to the relationship of a coach and athlete:

> …teachers in these classrooms read student portfolios in the same way coaches view videotapes of their players, with an eye to improving performance through better coaching. They have a vested interest in the success of their student writers and read portfolios, in part, to discover the strengths and weaknesses of the learning environment they have created for individual students and for the class as a whole. (121)

A well-written portfolio potentially benefits you and your instructors alike.

Effects on Program

Individual Course Portfolios usually have little impact on a college or university program because of their narrow scope. Student Career Portfolios have somewhat more influence because they potentially serve as job-seeking tools and thus reflect on the successful training of graduates.

The Program Assessment Portfolio helps your instructors and/or college or university administrators determine how effectively you have been taught. For this reason alone, it is vital that you submit an appropriate portfolio so that the administrators can decide whether or not the course is covering the right material, if it is covering that material effectively, and if students' portfolio presentation skills are appropriate for the level of the course. In such assessment, students' names are generally kept confidential. It is the program that is being evaluated, not you (though, in some cases, as we have just discussed, your grade can be affected). The long-term impact of such portfolios is that the results can positively affect the curriculum; future students will see improved instruction as a result of your portfolio work!

Types of Portfolios

Whether or not your portfolio is for one instructor's class or for your entire program of study, you may be asked to submit one of two particular types of portfolios or some combination of them.

Growth Portfolios

Some portfolios reveal how much growth your writing exhibited during the course, so that early, weaker pieces are contrasted with the more mature writing done at the end of the term. Such a portfolio is called a "developmental portfolio" (Lankes 1) or "process portfolio" (D'Aoust 40) or "comprehensive portfolio" (Weiser 94) or "working portfolio" (Yancey 108). Generally, a growth portfolio includes every draft of a limited number of papers to show evidence of your writing development. Some growth portfolios require you to include a weak paper and explain why it did not "work." Instructors using these portfolios will be looking to see if they can trace improved knowledge and writing mastery.

Final Portfolios

Other instructors will want you only to show your very best pieces in what's called a "showcase portfolio" (Lankes 2) or "exemplary portfolio" (D'Aoust 40) or "selected portfolio" (Weiser 94) or "completed or final portfolio" or "presentational portfolio" (Yancey 108). Final portfolios generally include only the final or best draft of each assignment, with several assignments usually included.

A broader type of final portfolio offers course credit for life or past experience. In such a case, students will want to ensure the contents of the portfolio are clearly presented, thorough, and pertinent. While the portfolio might be complimented by exam results, interviews, or timed writing samples, the portfolio itself often serves as a more permanent, tangible proof of your work and thus, at least subconsciously if not tacitly, takes on extended significance.

Merged Portfolios

Faculty might ask you to submit a portfolio that combines elements of the growth and final portfolios. For instance, you may be asked to include one paper with multiple drafts and accompanying materials but only final drafts of a select number of other papers. Student career portfolios often require merged portfolios.

Knowing which type of portfolio you are compiling can greatly affect your final product. Regardless of portfolio type, getting a portfolio "right" can often make the difference in its success.

Goals of Portfolios

Just as there are many types of portfolios, there are also a variety of goals common to most portfolios. While you may be tempted to compile the portfolio with only one goal in mind—get it done to get a grade—you might also consider the advantages and opportunities which properly completing a portfolio offers you. Eckerd College faculty have stated that portfolios offer students the ability to "…claim ownership and authority over their writing, to review the papers they have written in college, to decide which ones they think are best, and to articulate their writing strengths" (Harrison 45). The process of collecting a portfolio promises to help you develop in several ways.

Reflecting Improved Writing Skills

For composition and other writing-intensive courses, instructors will primarily be concerned as they grade portfolios with changes in your writing evident at the sentence, paragraph, and essay levels. If their comments to you have mentioned that your writing does not display a mastery of certain sentence-level conventions, then it will be imperative that you learn about and correct those problems since including such problems in your writing suggests that your work is not quite college-level material. While an occasional slip at any point in your college career might be understandable or a pattern of one "error" type might appear in your early drafts as a result of past insufficient writing instruction, not fixing these problems is seen as unforgivable by most instructors. Consult Chapter 3 for more information on successfully revising these problems.

Your portfolio will need to prove mastery of sentence-level errors in order to be successful, but stopping with just those improvements will not ensure portfolio success. Too many students feel that simply correcting their "mistakes" equals portfolio revision. However, you must also consider (and you should do this first) paragraph-level and overall problems and revise accordingly, as recommended in Chapter 3.

Reflecting a Polished Presentation Style

In addition to writing skills, instructors also examine the appearance of your portfolio. While an attractive portfolio with meticulously prepared cover sheets and title pages cannot compensate for weak writing and lack of content, paying attention to the presentation style of your portfolio does remain important.

The portfolio should be neat, self-contained, and complete. Section tabs, cover pages, table of contents pages and other organizational devices provide instructors with helpful information; though they are not always required, their addition helps the instructor navigate your portfolio and understand more about your work ethic and personality. The appearance and, especially, writing style of your reflection statement (see Chapter 5) also help to demonstrate your maturity and professionalism as a student. In general, HOW you present the portfolio can send subtle (and, when done poorly, not-so-subtle!) messages to your instructor about how important you perceive the course to be, about how he or she should view your work, and about your overall success in the course.

Reflecting Knowledge Imparted

This particular goal of a portfolio is significant for all of the types and goals of portfolios. Individual Course Portfolios should exhibit content-based data gained during the course. Especially in content courses such as in the sciences or the humanities, showing that you understand the major concepts of the course is an important component of the portfolio. Even in courses devoted solely to writing, portfolios that engage with the material that was read and discussed and with the content devoted to writing instruction prove to the instructor that you have acquired the knowledge presented in the course.

It is also important for portfolios designed to assess a program to reflect certain core information that all students taking that course or that program should master. Sometimes, for these portfolios, your best work in terms of grades might not show the breadth of the knowledge you gained as much as papers or projects on which you scored lower do. Indeed, if you were grappling with difficult content, you might have devoted less attention to the writing or the presentation of that particular paper. Still, that piece may reflect the type of information gained more than a paper or project where you wrote well but covered less or old material. Thus, it becomes very important in meeting the goals of a Program Assessment or Student Career Portfolio that you carefully examine the requirements of the portfolio (see Chapter 4). Merely providing "A" papers sometimes is less helpful in assessing how much you learned than providing insightful work is.

Audiences for Portfolios

Now that you know more about why portfolios are written, you need to consider exactly who will be reading this portfolio. Even though the obvious audience for a course portfolio is the instructor, other less-obvious audiences exist.

You as an Audience Member

You become the initial judge of a portfolio's success, and—depending on whether you are a perfectionist or a slacker, whether you have allowed ample time or not, and whether or not you understand what other audience members seek from the portfolio—your estimation of its worth may very well be accurate. Nonetheless, whether or not you are satisfied with the work will often depend on intangible factors relating to your interest in the course, in school altogether, your outside work and social responsibilities, and, perhaps most importantly, your attitude about writing or other skills required in the portfolio. These factors may alter the writing, presentation, and content of a portfolio, but stepping outside your daily environment to examine your portfolio work objectively can be difficult.

Throughout this text, you will be reminded to move steadily and efficiently through the steps required in the portfolio because the single most important way to ensure your satisfaction with the finished portfolio is to allow enough time to complete it, to put it aside for a time, and then to revise it one last time. Doing so will not only leave you with a product to be proud of, but it will also better satisfy the other potential audience members.

Family and Friends

In the past, you may relied solely on those closest to you for advice about your writing. Classmates may be asked to serve as peer reviewers for parts of the portfolio, but, just as often, you may ask your roommates, friends, or family members to "check over" papers. Having multiple readers can give you a variety of perspectives and responses to your writing; the old adage about two heads being better than one has merit. Be sure, however, that your outside readers fully understand the assignments. Otherwise, their advice may contradict what the instructor seeks from you.

Instructors or Program Administrators

Sometimes, despite the written and/or oral instructions that professors or programs gave, you may have depended more on what you thought instructors would want than on the techniques or tips they provided. Admittedly, many instructors are less than clear about what they expect from an assignment or from a portfolio; sometimes, they never articulate at all how you should best accomplish the tasks set out before you. If your instructor is not clear, ask for clarification. If, as is sometimes the case, he or she seems reluctant or unable to clarify what is expected, then visit the writing center on campus with assignment in hand. Frequently, the tutors there will have seen similar assignments and can help you better understand what the professor is seeking. Notice any positive samples provided by the instructor; these should be clues as to how he or she wants the finished product to look or to read, just as negative samples offer clear-cut evidence of what is not successful. Generally, college professors are less impressed with fancy presentation and million-dollar words than clarity, precision, and thoroughness.

Other Faculty and Administrators

If the portfolio is for program assessment or represents your academic career, your portfolio will probably be submitted to other faculty or administrators—perhaps administrators from other schools—to evaluate in terms of program goals. Again, writing and presentation will be important, but the portfolio's content will often drive their reading of the portfolios so that they may ask as they go whether or not the portfolio meets the minimum standards they have agreed on in terms of knowledge about the subject.

If the portfolio seems to be lacking in some element of the course's curriculum, then they may assume that you somehow missed that portion of the course or that your selections in the portfolio merely do not include that information. However, when they begin to notice such vacuums in other students' work, whether it is across an individual class or the entire program, then they start questioning the effectiveness of a given professor or the entire program relative to that particular missing material.

Your Individual Course Portfolio may also be read by outside readers in the event you appeal a grade or if your instructor cites examples of your work in his or her research or portfolios. (They really should get your permission in writing before doing the latter.) In either case, you want the portfolio to be a positive reflection of you as a student for posterity's sake.

Future Employers

Fields such as art, photography, advertising, and modeling have long-standing traditions of asking prospective employees to provide samples of their work. Increasingly, employers in other fields want verifiable proof of your abilities to communicate in written and spoken discourse. Portfolios provide evidence of half of those abilities. Employers will want evidence that you have mastered the content of your field, that you communicate well, and that you have a sophisticated presentation style capable of positively reflecting their organization. When your portfolio reflects work from a major or capstone course, it can be especially crucial in securing your first job.

Role of the Instructor or Program Administrator

The professor's obvious roles in portfolio-based courses are to assign the portfolio, collect the portfolio, and evaluate the portfolio. If the portfolio assesses a program, then the administrator secures outside evaluators and compiles the numerical data. Regardless of type, professors will sometimes conduct portfolio workshops in class and/or individual or small group conferences about portfolios. Use this time efficiently by working on the portfolio beforehand and then coming prepared to such events with specific questions about your portfolio.

You should expect faculty to answer your questions (unless you become relentless in your questioning) regarding the content or portfolio. If you are still unclear, again, visit your writing center to help clarify what you need to do or, as a last resort, visit your student ombudsman or student services office to explain your inability to find answers concerning this very important project.

Your Role

The bulk of the work, of course, lies squarely on your shoulders, and, ultimately, the course grade you receive will be impacted by the portfolio. Thus, you must start early, work methodically and intelligently, and meet target deadlines. This text will help you do those things. At the end of each chapter, complete the final activity to ensure you are applying the guidelines to your own portfolio.

Complete the following chart as it relates to your own portfolio; then, start developing strong writing and other habits as you work, which is the focus of Chapter 2.

Assessing Your Portfolio Type

What is the goal of the portfolio you are compiling?

↔

**Individual Course
Portfolio**
↓
What percentage is the
portfolio worth? ____%

Student Career Portfolio
↓
Is submitting the portfolio
necessary for entry to or exit
from a specific program on
campus? Yes No

Program Assessment Portfolio
↓
Can the portfolio affect
your grade or graduation? Yes No

Is the portfolio designed to show
➤   Your growth as a writer?
➤   Your polished final writing?
➤   Both growth and polish?

**Name the specific audience member(s)
for your portfolio.**

What is the deadline for your portfolio?

Sketch out a rough timeline for its completion.

Works Cited

Arter, Judith A., Vicki Spandel, and Ruth Culham. *Portfolios for Assessment and Instruction.* Greensboro, NC: ERIC Digest, 1995. ED 388890. 2/1/2000.
http://www.ed.gov/databases/ERIC_Digests/ed388890.html

Callahan, Susan. "Portfolio Expectations: Possibilities and Limits." *Assessing Writing* 2.2 (1995): 117-151.

D'Aoust, Catherine. "Portfolios: Process for Students and Teachers." *Portfolios in the Writing Classroom: An Introduction.* Ed. Kathleen Blake Yancey. Urbana, IL: NCTE, 1992. 39-48.

Decker, Emily, George Cooper, and Susanmarie Harrington. "Crossing Institutional Boundaries: Developing an Entrance Portfolio Assessment to Improve Writing Instruction." *Journal of Teaching Writing* 12.1 (1992): 83-104.

Harrison, Suzan. "Portfolios Across the Curriculum." *WPA* 19 (1995): 38-48.

Lankes, Anna Maria D. *Electronic Portfolios: A New Idea in Assessment.* Syracuse, NY: ERIC Digest. 1995. ED 390377. 2/1/2000.
http://www.ed.gov/databases/ERIC_Digests/ed390377.html

Sheckley, Barry G. and Morris T. Keeton. "Perspectives on Key Principles of Adult Learning." *CAELforum and News* 21.3 (Spring 1998): 3-5, 34.

Sroda, Sue. "Final Portfolio Guidelines." ENG 324-01 Fall 1999 Syllabus. Murray, KY: Murray State University.

Tully, Marianne. *Helping Students Revise Their Writing.* New York: Scholastic Professional Books, 1996.

Weiser, Irwin. "Portfolio Practice and Assessment for Collegiate Basic Writers." *Portfolios in the Writing Classroom: An Introduction.* Ed. Kathleen Blake Yancey. Urbana, IL: NCTE, 1992. 89-100.

Wilson, Lisa M. "Portfolio Self-Evaluation." ENG 101-32 Fall 1999 Syllabus. Murray, KY: Murray State University.

Yancey, Kathleen Blake. "Portfolios in the Writing Classroom: A Final Reflection." *Portfolios in the Writing Classroom: An Introduction.* Ed. Kathleen Blake Yancey. Urbana, IL: NCTE, 1992. 102-116.

Chapter 2
Develop Good Writing Habits Now

"It's good to write clearly, and anyone can"
(Joseph M. Williams 4).

Do any of these traits characterize your writing?

➢ Do you delay writing until the last minute?

➢ Do you worry as you write about your spelling, mechanics, etc.?

➢ Do you view writing as a solitary, boring activity?

➢ Do you avoid using ideas from outside sources in your writing?

➢ Do you forget about a project once you finish the first version?

This chapter will help you modify your writing skills so they are more conducive to a portfolio-based writing approach.

If you arrived at your university or college without strong writing skills, you may have found yourself at an extreme disadvantage, but even you were a successful writer in high school, you may have become dismayed at the sheer volume of writing and reading required in college. In order to produce good writing not only in the portfolio but also throughout your academic and professional career, start now to develop coping and stylistic strategies that you might not have been formerly taught.

Some students mistakenly believe that portfolio preparation resembles cramming for a final exam. However, neither students nor instructors are generally pleased with portfolios that receive little forethought. If a portfolio deadline looms at the end of a course, the best time to begin revising the portfolio happens to be as you write the initial draft; you can forestall many problems often associated with portfolios simply by submitting better, more exact writing as a first draft. This chapter will give you some concrete advice about improving your writing strategies—strategies that can save you time and effort and, overall, make writing much less of a chore than it might currently be for you.

Avoid Procrastination

We all, admittedly, suffer moments—or longer periods of time—when we would rather do virtually anything than start writing. Nonetheless, the actual writing often proves to be less onerous than the fear of starting. Writing becomes far less burdensome when it is approached in discrete steps and well in advance of due dates. Start early on the individual assignments that comprise the portfolio. If you suffer from true "writer's block," then you might consult your course handbook, your university's writing center, or the Susan Palo text listed in the Works Cited section at the end of this chapter. Most of what students call "writer's block," however, can be readily solved by a few simple strategies:

- **Write about something you are interested in** when assignments allow.

- **Approach a writing task with a goal of learning**. Too often, writers assume that putting words on paper means tedium. Instead of thinking about writing as revealing only what you know or have just researched, think of writing as an opportunity to explore new perspectives about a subject.

- **Remove distractions**. Recall those times in the past when your writing flowed and you were successful in completing a writing task in a timely manner. Try to recreate the writing conditions that fostered such success. Some writers need silence to perform well; others feel they need music or television playing in the background. Figure out how you write best and frequently create opportunities for yourself to write in just such conditions. As your academic calendar gets fuller, you may find that time will not allow the luxury of only writing in optimal conditions. Many people find they must write whenever and wherever the opportunity strikes—while riding a bus, between classes, etc. Understand that, in the initial writing stages, getting the ideas down becomes the crucial focus, whether you are scribbling down some rough ideas while waiting for a conference with your instructor or curling up in your favorite chair at home while writing a masterpiece.

- **Begin where you left off.** One effective strategy employs turning off your writing flow just before all words dry up. Simply stop a bit early once you do start writing and then list your next idea in just enough words to remind you what you intended to say. That way, you will not have to face a blank page when you return to your text.

- **Tape yourself.** Many writers who enjoy verbal fluency but who cannot seem to get those same eloquent words on paper benefit from "talking" a paper onto an audio or videocassette. The words then have to be transcribed, but some students who dread starting writing find this helpful.

- **Use traditional prewriting strategies.** Many handbooks and course texts such as *The Access Handbook* by laGuardia and Guth or *The Longwood Guide to Writing* by Lunsford and Bridges feature activities geared to help writers overcome procrastination: clustering, freewriting, brainstorming, cubing, and asking certain questions are among the most popular.

Not all of these techniques work for all writers; experiment with them to find the one that best suits your writing style.

Think Globally First

Once you get started, you may wonder what needs attention first. While it is possible to start with the introduction and write straight through to the conclusion, all the while focusing exacting attention to all of the mechanical and grammatical elements of a sentence, you may find this strategy ineffective. Often, such writing results in essays that divert from their original intent or say very little fresh information. One strategy you might try is to construct your main ideas first—develop and expand them until you have covered the important points that you wanted to share with your readers. Then, devise an introduction and conclusion that direct readers into and out of the essay—a beginning and ending that clearly reflect what you actually cover.

If you suffer anxiety about perfecting every sentence before moving on, then try this: Darken the computer screen or cover the page. Students who suffer from procrastination because they tend to overedit as they write often find it helpful NOT to look at what they just wrote. The simple act of physically removing the words from sight thus frequently results in less frustration with writing. When you get your ideas formed in writing, then you can begin refining them.

Develop an Active Writing Style

If, as you write your initial drafts, you will adopt some active writing strategies, your portfolio revisions will be less cumbersome.

- **Engage yourself in your writing**. Be an active reader in your own writing process by asking questions and taking notes about necessary research as you go. As you make statements, question "Why?" or "How?" If you can explain the answers, then do so, at least initially. Many students do not provide enough background support for their ideas, so the more you anticipate readers' questions and provide the background they need, the more helpful your text will become. Also, note to yourself those areas where you need further support that you are not able to provide on your own.

- **Use active language**. One of the hallmarks of a sophisticated writing style is the use of vivid, active language. While you could defer a focus on your actual word choice until revision, a conscious effort to substitute words—especially verbs that indicate little action, such as *am, are, is, was, were, have, can,* etc.—with more active, interesting words—verbs such as *ran, thought, considered, existed,* etc.—can make an immediate impact on your writing style. If you find that fretting over such words stifles your writing, simply highlight the less active words and return to them during revision.

- **Engage others with your writing**. Take advantage of peer revision or pre-draft conferences with your instructor to engage others in determining appropriate content and support for your points. Be prepared with specific questions, not just about spelling, etc., but about whether or not a point you are including makes sense or needs more explaining. This will give you specific feedback from an outside reader before you actually submit the work.

Conduct Background Research Thoroughly

When you consult outside research to supplement your own ideas in a piece of writing, your writing promises to be better supported and more insightful. As you conduct the research, you must be thorough, not only in ensuring that you not take the writer's words out of context simply to provide support for your own ideas, but also in compiling a complete record of every source you use. Be sure to keep up with which author said exactly what and on what exact page; to do otherwise might result in plagiarism, which is a serious academic offense. Keep up also with the entire publishing information for every article or book you use. Handbooks provide models for how to cite your sources properly; be sure to consult your assignment, syllabus, or instructor about the appropriate citation style—the most commonly used include MLA, APA, and Chicago. Your instructor may have additional information to include, such as a reference number.

Compiling your works cited or reference page as you go ensures that you do not leave out texts and is much less tiresome than creating it "after the fact." Many word processing software programs will automatically format the works cited page for you so that you simply have to enter the data into the proper location.

If you need statistical data or visuals to complete your project, begin now to compile and develop them. Keep accurate records of your sources for the data or visuals. Begin to work now with your computer software if you plan to develop tables, charts, or graphs. Also, don't neglect to include headings and proper identifications of the data and visuals.

Start Reflecting

Just as it is wise not to wait until the last minute to begin your actual assignments or portfolio revisions, it is also smart to begin reflecting now, long before the actual reflection statement is due. You might wonder how you can do that without an actual assignment for the reflection statement in hand. While you may eventually discard some of your early material, getting in the habit and the mindset of critiquing your writing will help prepare you for whatever is required on the actual reflection assignment. Start by jotting down your reactions to each paper as soon as it is complete.

- What did you learn about the subject that you did not previously know?

- What did you learn about your writing style?

- What did you learn about constructing this particular type of assignment?

- What are the features of this piece about which you are particularly proud?

- What do you see as its weaknesses?

Writing such responses now will give you a record of your initial reaction to the piece and will allow you to chart your growth as a writer when you begin the revision process.

Your Role

Writing is a multi-faceted process and current research indicates that no one writer engages in the same steps in the same order at the same time as any other writer. Your job early on in a project as important and complicated as a portfolio is to understand how you write, what keeps you from writing, and in what ways your writing needs to improve.

Assessing Your Writing Habits

1. Do you frequently suffer from procrastination or writer's block?
    Yes...Go to question 2.
    No...Try removing distractions or incorporating creative ways to get your ideas on paper.

2. Do you write best in certain environments?
    Yes...Go to question 3.
    No...Try establishing a particular place, time, attitude, and sequence for your writing.

3. Are you easily distracted by grammar or mechanical problems as you write first drafts?
    No...Go to question 4.
    Yes...Try covering your writing as you go or merely underlining areas that need attention when you are finished composing.

4. Do you act as an active reader of your own work?
    Yes...Go to question 5.
    No...Try asking yourself questions to ensure you have covered the topic from all angles.

5. Have you adequately researched your topic?
    Yes…Go to question 6.
    No…Try using multiple sources without relying on one source or
        one type of source too much.

6. Do you feel confident in how you organize your writing?
    Yes…Go to question 7.
    No…Try using a variety of outlines, paragraph organization
        schemes, and/or inductive versus deductive methods until you
        find one appropriate for a particular piece of writing.

7. Do you write about the strengths of the essay once it is complete?
    Yes.
    No…Try reflecting on the essay's strength and
        weakness now while it is still fresh.

Works Cited

laGuardia, Dolores and Hans P. Guth. *The Access Handbook.* Needham
        Heights, MA: Allyn & Bacon, 2000.
Lunsford, Ronald F. and Bill Bridges. *The Longwood Guide to Writing.*
        Needham Heights, MA: Allyn & Bacon, 2000.
Palo, Susan. "An Interview with Mike Rose: 'Imagine a Writing
        Program." *Writing on the Edge* 1.2 (Spring 1990): 7-22.
Williams, Joseph M. *Style: Ten Lessons in Clarity and Grace.* 5th ed.
        New York: Longman, 1997.

Chapter 3
Understand Re(en)vision of Your Work

"We no longer assume that good writers are people capable of producing polished work on their first try; we know that writers do not often 'get it right' the first time" (Weiser 100).

As you prepare to revise your work, ask yourself:

➢ Why do instructors require revision for portfolios?

➢ What is revision?

➢ What is editing?

➢ How do the two differ?

This chapter will help you plan a revision strategy for your portfolio.

You and your instructors may differ drastically in defining the term "revision." For you, it might mean "cleaning up"—the grammar, the mechanics, and any other sentence-level problems referred to in the instructor's response to the paper. While these features must indeed be considered for the portfolio, to limit portfolios this narrowly may threaten your portfolio grade. As one educator points out, "...it's not about fixing errors, but about making their meaning clear" (Tully 8). Another instructor, Sue Sroda, warns students: "You won't get credit for just 'fixing' grammatical errors and the like. You need to rethink each document as a whole and see how it can be made better." Instructors define the term "revision" by its literal meaning—to see again. This thinking of revision as re-envision may help you understand the more global possibilities the instructor imagines the portfolio as having.

View Revision as an Opportunity

Indeed, re-envisioning a whole piece of writing and THEN revising it sentence by sentence sounds like a lot of work—not only in terms of physically writing or typing new ideas and corrections but also, and perhaps most significantly, in developing new perspectives on a piece of writing that you already felt you had exhausted. As Marianne Tully admits, ". . .revising is the hardest part of the process for the kids to do and for the teachers to teach" (6).

The amount of work you invest, however, can usually be directly related to the quality of the portfolio you wind up with. Many students submit portfolios that merely correct spellings and typos, and, for such minimal effort, instructors have little compelling force to elevate the student's grade. Such inaction by students leads instructor Christopher Burnham to comment, "Irresponsible revision occurs when students are doing only as much as they must to get by" (130). In fact, many instructors require students to highlight physically the changes made to the new text simply to show the relative amount of work devoted to the revision. In such instances, you will have an even more compelling reason to impress your instructor—not with padding but with new insights—and to challenge yourself to arrive at new, fresh angles on your topic. If you don't think of revision in such a way, you may lose "...the opportunity to extend the piece and make it even better, and...the chance to grow as a writer and a thinker," according to Tully (8).

With the immediacy that word processing offers in the restructuring of an essay via cut and paste, you are now given the opportunity of relatively easy revision that your academic ancestors did not enjoy just fifteen years ago. Revision throughout most of the history of American education was a physically labor-intensive and tedious process—when, indeed, it was allowed at all. Think of revision, then, as the opportunity to merge your growing understanding of your writing style with the instructor's recommendations to create a product you are really proud to claim as your own.

Understand Instructors'
Recommendations for Change

Just as all writers write differently, all instructors respond uniquely to student writing. Frequently, students do not understand the importance of de-coding instructor comments before they revise. Christopher Burnham warns,

First, students generally do not comprehend written teacher responses. Second, when students do comprehend the comments, they generally do not know how to use them. And third, when students do use the comments, they do not necessarily produce more effective writing. (125)

To produce a final document that makes everyone happier, you might consider how your instructor serves as audience for the portfolio.

Many programs insist that instructors use standardized grading scales and holistic grading rubrics in an effort to limit wide variations in grading and to ensure conformity across all sections of a course. Programs that use portfolios for assessment frequently insist that instructors *not* grade the final portfolios for their own classes to provide objective outside readers for those texts and thus to contain wild excesses in grading. Once you receive feedback from an instructor, especially if the accompanying grade is much lower than you expected, you are well advised to find out what that number means—both within the class and within the program. Such information can be determined anecdotally from students who have taken the same instructor or the same course in that program. Sometimes, writing center tutors can give you an idea of the relative merit of your grade if they have seen a lot of papers from that instructor; do not ask them to give their evaluation of the grade, however, since other factors they may not be aware of may be affecting your grade.

Most importantly, the instructor can provide valuable information about both the grade and the comments; schedule a conference with the instructor after you have carefully reviewed the comments. Being emotional or argumentative will only upset both of you, so go into such a conference with specific, positive questions about what you can do to improve the paper for the portfolio.

Many instructors and programs do not give grades with portfolios, merely comments. This is an effort to alleviate concerns about grades. When this is the case, Weiser points out,

...students must consider the comments carefully, not only
because there is no grade on the paper, but also because the
comments provide them with suggestions for improving the
paper before it is submitted as part of the portfolio at the end
of the course. (93)

Some instructors write directly on your work or insert
comments within your text; others prefer to respond separately to your
work. Regardless of the approach the instructor chooses, the specific
language used can indicate your appropriate revision response. Some
instructors provide very few positive comments, focusing their limited
amount of time instead on what specific features need to be improved.
Others mark only grammatical errors; in such cases, ask the instructor
if he or she also expects content revision. Some will highlight
troublesome usage and mechanics by merely indicating the problems at
the end and expecting you to find and correct them (use a handbook!).
Others will simply say, "Proofread" or "Edit more carefully."
Especially when these words follow content comments, instructors
expect the proofreading to follow extensive global revision; editing
alone probably will not ensure success.

The instructor's comments may include a substantial number
of questions. For example, students in first-year composition classes
have received these comments:

- Was the reason for the divorce ever made clear to you? In
  retrospect, what sort of family life might you have had had they
  stayed together? (Did they realize it was a mistake later but were
  too proud to admit it or did they always fight like cats and dogs?)
  How did it impact your brother and sister? Can you see the impact
  in their lives?

- Expand the section about how little the girls did receive. Did they
  also receive less funding as a team for their sport? Less crowd
  support from the community?

Or the comments may include statements:

- Organization seems to be the weakest area of your paper.

- I became confused about the paragraph about doing homework...it
  didn't seem to connect well enough with the rest of the piece.

- Overall, you might think about discussing how it really does show how stressful modern life has become when people don't reflect, or worse, don't have places in their memories they can reflect about.

Such responses usually indicate that an essay needs more details and support. In rarer instances, instructors may be indicating areas that seem unrelated to the main point and are suggesting that at least part of the text needs deleting. Think of the instructor's comments as a conversation with a very careful listener who is telling you by his or her quizzical looks or insistent questions which areas do not satisfy curiosity about your topic. If you do not understand the instructor's specific comments or how you might implement them—after you have carefully read through them and reviewed your essay—schedule an actual conversation with the instructor and remove all doubt before you start revising.

Adopt Global Revision Strategies

Look carefully at the instructor's comments to discover what appear to be the most pressing areas that need revision. For instance, words like "Overall" or "Most importantly" often signal the features that strike the instructor as needing most attention. An ongoing paradox that instructors are keenly aware of is that, if they provide positive comments about a paper, those words are inevitably followed by an explicit or implicit "but" or "however." Looking to that negative area to begin your portfolio can be another global starting point; just be sure not to eliminate the strong points as you revise. Also, identify areas you felt were problematic when you initially submitted the draft. Revision offers you the opportunity to question why those areas were not effective, to "fix" those areas, or to substitute a better passage altogether.

Starting the revision process with such global concerns will be a more efficient use of your time than correcting individual sentences first—sentences that might ultimately be deleted. Likewise, the new material you add will need deliberate revising and editing as well and will need to be incorporated into the flow of the current sentences; consequently, the old sentences may need transitions added to help your writing be more cohesive.

In addition to thinking globally, revisit the other writing habits you developed as you wrote the initial draft now that you are ready to revise it:

- **Do not delay** the revision process. As soon as the paper is returned, start tackling the draft in stages to allow ample time for your ideas to develop and to avoid last-minute panic.

- **Write actively** in response to the instructor's questions, noting not only your own reactions but also possible areas that might need further research.

- **Conduct additional research** as soon as possible, being sure to cite and record any new sources.

- **Expand on ideas** by providing new data, new quotes from experts, new examples, anecdotes, or other supporting material.

- **Provide transitions** between the new and old material.

- **Ask** a classmate or writing center tutor to read the new draft and respond to its revised contents.

- **Compare** this new working draft with your original submission. If they look very similar and you received anything less than an A on the paper, then you probably can do more to improve it.

Reflect on the writing in light of the new insights you develop now that you have an "official" reader response to your work. Ask yourself what the instructor's comments highlight that you "should have thought of." Actually write down responses to these questions:

- What was recommended that you would have never considered? Why would it have not occurred to you?

- What have you learned about the amount and type of support necessary to get your points across to a reader?

- What do you need to know more about relative to proofreading/editing?

Develop Stronger Editing Skills

Because the writing in a portfolio represents the best product you are capable of producing at this given point in your academic career, attention to detail often indicates a level of maturity and an understanding of academic prose that can set your portfolio apart from less polished products. Again, actually revising sentence-by-sentence should come last in the writing process. As Tully states,

> In the classroom, when we refer to editing as part of the steps of the writing process, we usually think of it as the last stage before making a final copy for publishing. Editing is the step that does not usually change the content of the piece; it usually corrects the pieces for conciseness, accurate spelling and usage. (83)

Once you are sure of the content, then start eliminating errors, especially the types of errors indicated by the instructor's comments. (Remember, new errors often creep into the expanded material.)

Look also for those error types that mark unsophisticated writing. The most significant "errors" include the following:

- Comma splices

- Run-ons (or fused sentences)

- Sentence fragments

- Tense shifts

- Faulty subject-verb agreement

- Faulty pronoun reference.

Outside readers can be helpful in identifying these and other grammatical or mechanical errors. Visit your campus writing center or ask a trusted friend who is a skilled writer to help you detect errors after you have found all you can. Do not, however, rely solely on others. Some may have outdated, misguided, or simply wrong understandings of how language works. Consult your handbook frequently, and do not hesitate to visit your campus writing center; do not ask or expect the tutors, though, to "proofread" your papers. Many will simply refuse, feeling that, if they edit the paper for you, it would not help you understand the problems you might be having with your writing. In cases where you receive conflicting information, ask your instructor. The final drafts in your portfolio need to be as polished as possible. After all, as Burnham points out, once teachers read the finished portfolio, "Definitions, revisions, and arguments must be considered for what they are, rather than what they could be after revisions" (133).

Your Role

Instructors who read a lot of portfolios can immediately identify those portfolios that have received careful attention and whose authors genuinely responded to the revision process. If your revised papers merely mirror the originals (and instructors frequently compare the two drafts), you may leave the instructor disappointed that you have ignored critical advice which could have dramatically improved the paper and, in doing so, given you and potential audience members fresh insight into the topic. Take revision seriously, and the rewards will be both intrinsic and real.

Revising Your Writing

First, ask yourself:

What problem areas did you find with the paper?

What problem areas did your peer reviewers find with the paper?

What problem areas did your professor find with the paper?

In what areas do these responses coincide?

Why are these problem areas problematic?

What are the key terms that identify the global recommendations made in your professor's comments?

Now, follow these steps:

Be sure you understand the professor's comments.
Attack global ideas, especially those
needing new research, first.
Provide transitions between
new and old material.
Edit the entire text.
Get a review.

Works Cited

Burnham, Christopher C. "Portfolio Evaluation: Room to Breathe and Grow." *Training the New Teacher of College Composition.* Ed. Charles W. Bridges. Urbana, IL: NCTE, 1986. 125-138.

Sroda, Sue. "Final Portfolio Guidelines." ENG 324-01 Fall 1999 Syllabus. Murray, KY: Murray State University.

Tully, Marianne. *Helping Students Revise Their Writing.* New York: Scholastic Professional Books, 1996.

Weiser, Irwin. "Portfolio Practice and Assessment for Collegiate Basic Writers." *Portfolios in the Writing Classroom: An Introduction.* Ed. Kathleen Blake Yancey. Urbana, IL: NCTE, 1992. 89-100.

Chapter 4
Select Appropriate Material to Include

*"Although there is no single correct way to develop portfolio
programs, in all of them, students are expected to
collect, select, and reflect" (Sweet 2).*

As you gather your portfolio materials, consider these questions:

➤ What are the best papers you have written for this project? The
worst? Why?

➤ Do you need to show growth or polish or both in your portfolio?

➤ Do your best pieces necessarily show writing growth?

➤ For which type of portfolio might your weaker pieces be better
samples?

➤ Does your portfolio need to reflect a variety of content?

➤ How should you organize the portfolio?

Many times, it is not that the contents of portfolios are poorly
written that invalidates or reduces their grade. Rather, it is that they are
incomplete or they inaccurately represent the material. In essence, they
appear not to be missing the target but to be shooting at the wrong
target entirely. You may feel unsure about what to include in your
portfolio, especially if the instructor's assignment is unclear or general
in nature. Take heart, however, because you do already possess the
skills necessary to sift through your material critically. As Yancey and
Weiser point out about students, "They do exhibit a kind of expertise:
they *know* how they write, how they read, how they understand, what is
going on in their other classrooms, and their other schools and their
other lives" (16). Being sure that the material you include is appropriate
is crucial to the portfolio's success.

Suit Writing Selections to Portfolio Type

The type of portfolio you are writing may determine the types of material you should include. Edgerton, Hutchings, and Quinlan have pointed out that, "...the different understandings about what portfolios are, and the different ways they can be used, all have bearing on the determination of what a portfolio should contain" (7).

If you are writing an **Individual Course Portfolio,** you need to look carefully at the assignment to see

- if you have options in the number and selection of essays you include;

- or if all previously written essays MUST be revised;

- or if there are additional elements, such as a Reflection Statement, that need to be included.

Find out what, specifically, the instructor sees as the goal of the portfolio; most will value your re-envisioning your text while others will not accept portfolios with grammatical mistakes regardless of the extent of the content's revision. Some instructors ask for growth portfolios and will look to see how much improvement you have made in your content knowledge and/or writing style. Others want to see a final portfolio and will look only at the quality of the finished product to see if you have reached a benchmark standard for the course. Still others want to see a variety of types of writing, i. e, writing that serves multiple purposes for multiple audiences.

Student Career and **Program Assessment Portfolios** often require fewer pieces because greater numbers of students are submitting work, making the grading and storage load heavier. If you are writing a Program Assessment Portfolio, then you will need to consider these components of the portfolio process:

- How many and what types of pieces need to be included?
- What additional elements, such as a Reflection Statement, should be added?
- If required, what should the Reflection Statement reveal about the learning that took place?
- What is the minimum number of courses that must be represented?

- What should the pieces and the portfolio reflect overall about your learning?

This last question is vital to the assessment of a student's career or program. Too often, essays are included in portfolios that scored well or can be easily revised. However, program assessors are generally less concerned with being impressed with your individual performance than they are in seeing that specific instructional goals are reflected as having been met at some point in your program. This is especially true of content courses, rather than writing courses, so program administrators can immediately see whether or not instructors are covering appropriate material. Your instructor will, of course, be pleased if your writing not only reflects that the course material was thoroughly covered, but also presents that material with flair. This is especially important if your Student Career Portfolio also serves as an employment skills portfolio or if your Program Assessment Portfolio is also counted toward your course grade.

For all types of portfolios, you will need to find out whether or not the pre-writing notes, research notes, rough drafts, peer reviews, etc., are to be included in your portfolio; usually such items are included only in growth portfolios, but not always. Purdue University's Developmental Writing Program asks students to include all of the formal papers written during the term, "...including the required planning assignments, the drafts that have been read and critiqued by classmates, and the initial revision of each paper that has been read and responded to by the instructor" (Weiser 90). Other portfolios might include, "...excerpts from writing logs, from reader-writer journals, from other classes... nonscholastic writing..." or even "self-initiated writing" (Yancey 109).

Some instructors want you to include material that was not successful; Tom Romano explains why: "What writers consider not their best work—and the reasons why—can be just as informative about their aesthetic growth as their best writing and the stories about that writing" (155). Others do not want you to include unsuccessful materials, especially in a final portfolio, because that potentially puts your work in a negative light.

Knowing why you are including optional material or selecting among required texts becomes important. Donald Graves informs us,

> Even when students are allowed to decide which work belongs in their portfolios, the reasons for their decisions often seem

casual: "I'm choosing this one because it is about the Boston
Celtics." "I worked hard on that one; it's my longest one."
"This is better because it's about dogs, not cats." "This is my
research paper on the Civil War. My teacher gave it an A."
(85)

When you do have choice, knowing which essays to include and why
you are including them can make all the difference in your grade, but
you may not know how or why. Thus, Graves recommends starting
your selection process by acquainting yourself with what you value in
your writing:

Pick out two pieces
- that you just like.

- that you just wanted to keep writing.

- where you'd like to go back and rework the lines.

Pick out a piece
- that was just plain hard to write.

- where you might have said to yourself, "I think I'm
  getting the hang of this."

- where something surprised you during the writing....

- that...resembled your old way of writing.

- where you actually learned something about the event or
  information you were writing about. (Graves 93-94)

Once you have selected these pieces, begin to narrow them down to the
required number by finding those selections that you chose most
frequently.

Represent Your Varied Best

Once you understand exactly what has to be included in the
portfolio, then begin to decide which pieces meet the requirement.

Further narrow the possible pieces by identifying which ones meet the requirements yet reflect a sophisticated style and/or a mature, detailed handling of the subject matter. Portfolios that represent a broad range of genres or essay types further reveal your growth as a writer. If you are allowed a range of pieces or if the instructor allows you to include revisions of as many drafts as you want to include, do not interpret that as a blanket invitation to include everything. Be selective, choosing fewer pieces than the maximum, if necessary, rather than including more, but weaker, essays. For example, if the acceptable range includes three to five essays, then three strong essays are better than five essays if two are weak. Marianne Tully has presented a list of criteria for selecting finished writing:

- The writing piece is complete, presentable, and well organized.

- The writing is clear.

- The writing flows.

- The writing is appropriate for the audience.

- The purpose is fulfilled.

- The subject matter is important to the writer.

- Qualities of good writing are evident.

- The writing expresses the material creatively. (91)

If all of the essays from the course must be included in the portfolio, then work as you revise to insure that the pieces reflect variety in their style, organization, and topic. Just as the instructor does not want the final draft to look exactly like the first draft, neither does the instructor want every paper to mirror all the others in its approach. Indeed, the portfolio process aims to show your adaptability with the content and your fluidity with language.

Organize Your Portfolio

Yancey points to possible means for arranging the portfolio:
...by goals; by type of writing (for example, personal or
public, narrative or transactional, imaginative); by
chronological sequence; [or] by the writer's sense of
satisfaction with a piece or a piece's state of completion....
(109)

The assignment requirements, the type of course or program, and your
own preferences will determine your final choice.

Try to highlight your best pieces by placing them prominently
in the portfolio. In the front, they may positively influence the
instructor's opinion immediately. In the rear, they may leave the reader
with a strong, positive closing memory (especially with Program
Assessment Portfolios where a lot of papers are often evaluated in a
short period of time, and your paper needs to be especially memorable
to score well). The portfolio's table of contents and, to some extent,
the reflection statement should help make the organizational scheme
apparent to your reader.

Your Role

Even the best writing in the world is ineffective if it does not meet its target audience. Your responsibility as the author of the portfolio is to find out exactly what it needs to include. If at any point you are not sure what belongs in the portfolio or if you cannot decide between pieces, consult your instructor or a writing center tutor. (Be sure to take the assignment and all of the portfolio contents with you.) Decide which pieces should be included to make the portfolio both complete and strong. Organize the portfolio in the most appropriate way to accommodate both the assignment requirements and the reader's ease. The portfolio ultimately should represent your best possible effort.

Selecting Material to Include

Is your portfolio intended to show

➤ Your growth as a writer?

> Be sure to show multiple drafts that reflect the positive
> changes made in the essays. Explain those drafts in your
> reflections (see Chapter 5).

➤ Your increased content knowledge?

> Be sure the essays you include reveal significant content and a
> more sophisticated understanding of that knowledge in the
> latest pieces and/or revisions.

➤ What was taught in the course?

> Look over course notes and textbooks to ensure that your
> portfolio reflects broad coverage of the course content.

➤ Your polished writing?

> Select the pieces of writing that reveal a flexibility in writing
> style, logical and well-organized arguments, and cleanly
> edited final versions.

➤ All of the above?!

Must all essays be revised for the portfolio?

↔

Yes.	No.
↓	↓
How many and which essays are they?	How many may be included?
Find and revise them.	What types of essays best show your flexibility?
Can you organize them to put your best papers first?	What specific content knowledge or writing strategies must be reflected?
	Find the best selections; revise & organize them.

Are other elements required?

Yes.	No.
↓	↓
What other items must be included?	Be sure to include all the necessary essays.
Do they include a Reflection Statement?	Should you consider a cover or title page?
Compile the necessary elements.	

Works Cited

Edgerton, Russell, Patricia Hutchings, and Kathleen Quinlan. *The Teaching Portfolio: Capturing the Scholarship in Teaching.* AAHE Teaching Initiative of the American Association for Higher Education, 1991.

Graves, Donald H. "Help Students Learn to Read Their Portfolios." *Portfolio Portraits.* Eds. Donald H. Graves and Bonnie S. Sunstein. Portsmouth, NH: Heinemann, 1992. 85-95.

Romano, Tom. "Multigenre Research: One College Senior." *Portfolio Portraits.* Eds. Donald H. Graves and Bonnie S. Sunstein. Portsmouth, NH: Heinemann, 1992. 146-157.

Sweet, David. "Student Portfolios: Classroom Uses." *Office of Research Education Consumer Guide* No. 8, Nov. 1993. Office of Educational Research and Improvement, US Department of Education. 2/1/2000. http://www.ed.gov.pubs/OR/ConsumerGuides/classuse.html

Tully, Marianne. *Helping Students Revise Their Writing.* New York: Scholastic Professional Books, 1996.

Weiser, Irwin. "Portfolio Practice and Assessment for Collegiate Basic Writers." *Portfolios in the Writing Classroom: An Introduction.* Ed. Kathleen Blake Yancey. Urbana, IL: NCTE, 1992. 89-100.

Yancey, Kathleen Blake. "Portfolios in the Writing Classroom: A Final Reflection." *Portfolios in the Writing Classroom: An Introduction.* Ed. Kathleen Blake Yancey. Urbana, IL: NCTE, 1992. 102-116.

Yancey, Kathleen Blake and Irwin Weiser. "Situating Portfolios: An Introduction." *Situating Portfolios: Four Perspectives.* Eds. Kathleen Blake Yancey and Irwin Weiser. Logan, UT: Utah State UP, 1997. 1-17.

Chapter 5
Reflect on the Process

"Experience yields explicit knowledge only if reflected upon"
(Sheckley and Keeton 4).

Do you know...

➤ What the purposes of reflection statements are?

➤ How to highlight specific revisions you have made to a project?

➤ What your writing strengths are?

➤ What writing strategies you have learned as a result of the portfolio process?

➤ How important it is to present a polished reflection statement?

      If you have reflected on your writing throughout the composition and revision of each draft, the thought process behind—if not the actual writing of—reflections should begin to feel natural to you. If you have not analyzed your own writing before now, you may have a less concrete sense of what is involved. In either case, the reflection required in a portfolio becomes a major factor in the evaluation of that portfolio. This chapter provides specifics you should include as you reflect unless your instructor gives you a maximum amount of exact information he or she wants provided. Even then, the following information is frequently what the instructor seeks.

Understand the Importance of Reflection Statements

      Reflection statements reveal a great deal about you as their author. They indicate how seriously you have taken the assignment, how successful you are at understanding the assignment requirements, and how much attention to detail you devote to your work. In fact, some instructors consider the reflection statement crucial: "...the reflective writing is the most valuable part of the portfolio" (Decker, Cooper, and Harrington 90). Glenda Conway says reflection statements occupy a "privileged position" in most portfolios from the teacher's perspective:

> It is the cover letter that gets to speak the portfolio's first words, that portrays the character and the commitment of the writer, that conveys or appears to convey assumptions about the reader. It is the cover letter that has the most potential of all the portfolio documents to engage or alienate an audience. (83-84)

Despite the importance of reflection statements, you may be unsure how to reflect. For example, Catherine D'Aoust has found that "...most students lacked a vocabulary enabling reflection. They did not know what to say..." (44).

Unlike the initial drafts of each essay, the portfolio reflection statement rarely receives the benefit of revision suggestions from peers or instructors; thus, a strongly written reflection statement serves as a record of your current writing ability and/or fluency with the terminology from the class. In fact, instructors often can determine the strength of your portfolio revisions by simply reading the reflection statement. Since instructors are only human, such statements hold great, perhaps inordinate, impact over the instructor's reading of the actual portfolio revisions. A bland or uninformative reflection statement offers little to recommend either the portfolio or the learning that took place; it can also focus unwanted attention on the rest of the portfolio. For instance, composition instructors Decker, Cooper, and Harrington discovered at the University of Michigan that, "When poor reflective pieces raised questions in our minds about the students' competence, we looked more carefully at the other pieces in the portfolio to try to account for the relatively weak performance" (96).

Reflection statements can be written as cover letters, as Romano notes, "This is one of the major pieces of your work. The letter is your opportunity to explain, specifically, why you chose each piece to represent you. What made the pieces you chose stand out?" (150). Reflections can also appear as short reflection pieces that introduce or follow each individual piece within the portfolio. One of the most compelling aspects of well-written reflection statements is that they reflect the personality, or written voice, of the writer. Since you, ultimately, are the editor of the portfolio collection, the reflection statement offers the opportunity to reveal your own thought processes. Kirby and Kuykendall see this as an important step in learning: "We're convinced that students are nothing less than coauthors in this business of evaluating thinking. After all, it's their thinking" (194).

Point to Specific Changes

The more exact your reflection statement is about the changes you made in your writing, why you made them, and the results those changes made, the stronger your portfolio in general will be. Such specificity indicates that you have truly reflected on the work, and, without actually doing that nitty-gritty analyzing, your portfolio revision will not be substantially different or better anyway.

Many schools require quite exact information in the reflection statement; for instance, the cross-curricular campus-wide portfolio assessment program at Eckerd College in St. Petersburg, Florida has asked students to "...annotate each paper in their portfolios with a description of the circumstances of the writing, including the course assignment, the amount of time and number of drafts, and any assistance they received in writing" in addition to an overall reflective statement (Harrison 39). Lisa Wilson asks students to

> ...look at the first draft of the first paper you wrote this semester (or your worst draft), then compare it to the draft of the paper you thought was your best. How is it different? In actually writing the self-evaluation, you should mention which paper you thought was your best, and explain why in detail.

You should work to provide enough detail about the changes you have made. One student, for instance, submitted a reflection statement in a first-year composition course portfolio that begins, "I have made many changes to my papers. I have tried to make all changes that were suggested to me by my teacher" (MSU Student). The student does not, however, expand to reveal exactly what those changes were so that the reflection statement is so general that it becomes useless.

Another first-year student wrote, "My writing has almost certainly changed over the course of the past few months. When thinking back over the semester, I know my writing has changed, but I do not know specifically how" (MSU Student). Such a statement certainly leaves the instructor wondering if the instruction or the student was at fault in the student's inability to describe what happened to the writing.

On the other hand, if you are specific, the instructor is assured that true learning has occurred because you are beginning to self-diagnose your own writing problems. For example, another first-year student wrote, "In the HIV paper I provided smoother transitions from sentence to sentence; [sic] and I also made my thesis sentence a lot clearer. I combined more sentences, which also made the paper smoother, and I reworded sentences to where they were comprehendible" (MSU Student). Another student is even more specific:

> On page two, paragraphs two and three did not directly relate to each other until I added a transition sentence to connect the ideas that each contained. Another change that makes the paper easier to read was to change the word "currently" to "now" on page three, paragraph two. By using the introductory word "first" in the preceding sentence, I had set up the reader with the expectation that another series word would introduce the next point. I did not follow through with this, so the revision was clearly necessary. (MSU Student)

An advanced composition student wrote about the changes made in general to all papers in the portfolio:

> I re-vised (!) the papers by bettering the idea[s] as well as correcting some grammatical errors. These are the areas I focused on:
> - Transitions for subtle and logical flowing (for cohesion and coherence)
> - Adding detail
> - Deleting some information: as I add[ed] detail on some areas, some other areas needed to be shorter, or even completely deleted.
> - Forecasting the whole essay in the introductory part
> - Making sentences easier to understand: lessening nominalization, using "strong" verbs, removing unnecessary words, and etc.
> - Logical organization. (MSU Student)

Additional student examples are located in the Appendices, including Unsuccessful Reflection Statements (Appendix C), Good Reflection Statements (Appendix D), and Better Reflection Statements (Appendix E).

Highlight Strengths Identified by the Portfolio Process

Focus attention in your reflection statement on the development in your writing ability and/or your knowledge about the subject; this will provide your instructor with specific features to examine in your revisions. Such information helps reaffirm for the instructor whether or not his or her teaching has touched on the appropriate subjects or has helped you become a more critical thinker about the subject, about your writing, and, by extension, about the writing of others.

Again, statements that are generic in nature leave little information for the instructor to assess whether or not your writing has actually been strengthened. For example, one first-year student wrote (in a handwritten reflection statement hastily thrown into the portfolio on the day of submission),

> Throughout this class I've learn[ed] to look at not only the content of the paper but how it is writen [sic]. I've also learn[ed] to compare papers and how to look at all parts of the paper. I know I fixed all of my grammar error[s] and I enjoyed fixing the rest of [the] work but I don't know how well that went. (MSU Student)

Such a statement would make the instructor question whether or not the writing actually had improved (certainly the proofreading skills had not!).

On a more positive note, this student demonstrates how strength in student writing can be discussed:

> The main thing I have noticed as a growth in my writing throughout this past semester is my use of more complex sentences. I now utilize them more and better than before. Using them helps strengthen a paper by making it sound much less childish and more like thought was put into it. One of the other major things I've noticed improvements on in my writing is my use of commas. I used to be comma happy as

many students are[,] but I have come to know (at least more
than before) when and where to use them. (MSU Student)
Such statements move toward the goal professors have when assigning
reflection statements. For example, Sue Sroda requires the following
for her upper-level Technical Writing course portfolios:

A memo to me that introduces your portfolio's contents and
reflects over your work in the portfolio. You may want to
address things you learned, obstacles you overcame, and skills
learned over the course of the semester which you'll be able to
apply professionally.

Sroda clearly wants students to identify specifics that indicate what was
learned in the class. Glenda Conway wants her students to respect their
audience and "...to state claims and then to support those claims with
specific evidence" (88). Tully presents a short list of ideas that the
reflection statement might include:

How I have grown as a writer...
How I have met my goals in writing...
What I need to do next. (92)

The projection for the future of your writing introduces an element that
suggests you really are a writer interested not only in completing this
assignment, but also in furthering the skills you have learned in this
class in your future writings.

Comment on the Experience

In addition to pointing to specific revisions and to discussing
the overall features of your writing that have improved, it is often quite
appropriate to include your response to the entire process of portfolio
revisions, especially, or perhaps only, if that response seems positive.
Although students often want to, comments that border on flattery
about the instructor's teaching ability generally sound insincere. An
instructor does benefit, though, when you objectively report the
changes you have noticed in your writing and your critical thinking
abilities since originally writing your drafts. Such writing involves
"metacognitive work," according to Yancey (104).

Instructors also notice the comments you make about the
concrete lessons learned as you compiled the portfolio. Kirby and
Kuykendall have developed a list of questions that might help you in
this quest:

- What were the most difficult parts of the process?
- How did you go at this project? What were your work habits?
- What are you learning about your own processes as a writer...?
- How well did this approach to a final piece work for you? (191)

While instructors often rely more on student evaluations for such input, they often do include student reflection statements in their own teaching portfolios. Again, including such statements merely to flatter usually falls flat, but writing them to help you make sense of the course can be an effective element for including in your portfolio. Notice how this student is able to discuss the entire process and insert an implied compliment without compromising integrity:

> I have noticed substantial growth in my ability to write different forms of papers. I had never had to write anything more than a summary of a book before your class. I feel more confident in my abilities to write on demand now. In the future I hope to be able to improve even more on the effectiveness my writing has on the audiences I am writing for. (MSU Student)

Certainly, the instructor felt from reading this reflection statement that the portfolio process, the reflection statement, and the class itself had been a success.

Review the Reflection Statement

Strive to give the reflection statement the same careful attention that the rest of the portfolio receives. Because of its prominence within the portfolio, you are well advised to review it carefully. Tully tells students that, "At one point in the process, they need to stop being authors and to become readers and critics of their own work" (96).

As professor Sue Sroda examines the portfolios in her classes, she allows for the possibility that some papers are solid to begin with: "If you don't revise a document significantly, you can still get a very good grade by discussing how the document is perfect as it is and how the choices you initially made at every level...make it an excellent document." Bear in mind, however, that most instructors do not see "perfect" papers very often. Other instructors ask you to evaluate the approximate worth each paper should have within the portfolio—the percentage it should count (Chiseri-Strater 70). Still others ask you to self-assess the portfolio with a grade and then justify that grade.

As instructors evaluate reflection statements (and, indirectly, your entire portfolio), they frequently have preconceptions in their minds about what to expect from the portfolio statement; sometimes, they do not get what they expect. For instance, Glenda Conway says she was "disappointed" and "even insulted" by reflection statements that "appeared to have been written merely to fulfill an obligation":

> ...the disappointing letters were brief, general, and disengaging. On the surface they conveyed little or no sense of student self-reflection, while what seemed to be between the lines often spoke louder to me than what was present. These letters, in short, pushed the wrong "buttons." (86)

Conway further reminds us, "...the cover letter may be the only document in the entire portfolio that the teacher has not read some version of in the past...our only example of what our students can do on their own...that is addressed exclusively to the teacher" (89). To ensure the reflection statement's first impression is a strong one, you will, of course, want to edit the text carefully, and then ask someone else to review it just as you have probably done with your other papers. Careful proofreading and peer review of the reflection statement will ensure you have not made careless mistakes, thus giving the reflection statement itself the same polished appearance contained in the rest of the portfolio.

Your Role

The reflection statement, generally placed first in the actual portfolio, plays a deservedly prominent role in the instructor's understanding of that portfolio. The better able you are to show how the contents of the portfolio reveal your grasp of the significant aspects of the course, the better your portfolio will ultimately be (and the higher your portfolio will be evaluated). Pay special attention to proofreading and editing your reflection statement—at least as much as you do to the papers within the portfolio. Your reflection statement should be as unique as you are.

Reflecting on Your Writing

In what ways do your reflections reveal

➤ What makes your portfolio unique?

➤ What specific features of the class were beneficial in your learning?

➤ Your personal voice?

How do your reflections point to specific changes in

➤ The actual revisions in the portfolio?

➤ The improved knowledge you have gained?

➤ The growth you have made as a scholar?

Concerning the reflections, have you

➤ Revised to include all necessary components?

➤ Edited to ensure a polished appearance?

➤ Asked a peer reviewer or tutor to respond to it?

➤ Polished it for submission after final revisions?

Works Cited

Chiseri-Strater, Elizabeth. "College Sophomores Reopen the Closed Portfolio." *Portfolio Portraits*. Eds. Donald H. Graves and Bonnie S. Sunstein. Portsmouth, NH: Heinemann, 1992. 61-72.

Conway, Glenda. "Portfolio Cover Letters, Students' Self-Presentation, and Teachers' Ethics." *New Directions in Portfolio Assessment: Reflective Practice, Critical Theory, and Large-Scale Scoring*. Eds. Laurel Black, Donald Daiker, Jeffrey Sommers, and Gail Stygall. Portsmouth, NH: Boynton/Cook, 1994. 83-92.

D'Aoust, Catherine. "Portfolios: Process for Students and Teachers." *Portfolios in the Writing Classroom: An Introduction*. Ed. Kathleen Blake Yancey. Urbana, IL: NCTE, 1992. 39-48.

Decker, Emily, George Cooper, and Susanmarie Harrington. "Crossing Institutional Boundaries: Developing an Entrance Portfolio Assessment to Improve Writing Instruction." *Journal of Teaching Writing* 12.1(1992): 83-104.

Harrison, Suzan. "Portfolios Across the Curriculum." *WPA* 19 (1995): 38-48.

Kirby, Dan and Carol Kuydendall. *Mind Matters: Teaching for Thinking*. Portsmouth, NH: Boynton/Cook, 1991.

MSU Student. Samples from Professor Gina Claywell's ENG 101, 102, 104, and 404 Courses. Murray, KY: Murray State University. 1997- 1999.

Sroda, Sue. "Final Portfolio Guidelines." ENG 324-01 Fall 1999 Syllabus. Murray, KY: Murray State University.

Romano, Tom. "Multigenre Research: One College Senior." *Portfolio Portraits*. Eds. Donald H. Graves and Bonnie S. Sunstein. Portsmouth, NH: Heinemann, 1992. 146-157.

Sheckley, Barry G. and Morris T. Keeton. "Perspectiveson Key Principles of Adult Learning." *CAELforum and News* 21.3 (Spring 1998): 3-5, 34.

Tully, Marianne. *Helping Students Revise Their Writing*. New York: Scholastic Professional Books, 1996.

Wilson, Lisa M. "Portfolio Self-Evaluation." ENG 101-32 Fall 1999
    Syllabus. Murray, KY: Murray State University.
Yancey, Kathleen Blake. "Portfolios in the Writing Classroom: A Final
    Reflection." *Portfolios in the Writing Classroom: An
    Introduction.* Ed. Kathleen Blake Yancey. Urbana, IL: NCTE,
    1992. 102-116.

Chapter 6
Prepare the Actual Document

> *"In a portfolio I want you to present your best face."*
> *(Tom Romano 149).*

Before you submit your portfolio, you need to consider:

➤ What format must it be in?

➤ How can you make its contents clear?

➤ When and how should you protect your work?

Such considerations can save you time and effort and can help your portfolio be more successful.

The revisions are complete. The reflection statement clearly explains what you have learned. The course is almost over. Now, you are finally ready to compile the actual portfolio. Consult the assignment requirements and modify the following recommendations as necessary to fulfill your instructor's requirements. Sample student portfolio entries can be found in Appendix F to guide you as you complete your portfolio.

Physical Portfolio Submissions

Many instructors and programs may require you to submit actual portfolio folders. Knowing what type of portfolio folder to submit and its appearance are vital to the portfolio's success.

Follow Guidelines
If the instructions call for a specific folder type, be sure to invest in the proper type. Portfolio instructions often call for one of the following:

- A manila folder,
- An 8½" X 11"envelope,
- A pocket folder, or
- A hardbound or spiral folder.

Small portfolios might simply be stapled. Do not substitute if the instructions are clear; instructors have a range of reasons for requiring particular folder types, reasons ranging from the fact that some folders are too slippery or too thick to some folders allow material to fall out. If the instructions are not clear and the instructor never addresses the issue in class, then you might ask the instructor or former students about what works best.

Include the exact requirements in the order listed on the assignment. Some portfolios include a table of contents page. Reflection statements are then usually placed first. If the preferred order of the assignments themselves is not made clear, you may submit them in the order or the reverse order of how they were initially submitted or in the order of best to weakest papers. If the portfolio is for both program assessment and a course grade, check to see if the program assessment version should have only unmarked copies of the papers. Are there specific requirements about typing formats, font styles, font sizes, margins, etc.? If not, standard margins on word processing software are usually pre-set at an appropriate setting.

Check to see if you are to submit both new and old drafts (and all accompanying materials) or only the final drafts of each essay. If both drafts are to be included, instructors generally prefer to see the newest draft first. When possible, present your best work up front, which offers the very real possibility that instructors will be initially, even if subconsciously, impressed with your work (remember the old adage about first impressions!).

Introduce the Text

Do not rely on the reflection statement to carry the full weight of introducing your work. Providing a Table of Contents page or divider tabs for your portfolio helps the instructor know exactly where to find everything. (Short portfolios, of course, appear ridiculously overdone if the introductory features are longer than the portfolio!) At a very minimum, provide a cover sheet that identifies you, the date, the course, the instructor, and the fact that it is a portfolio. The assignment may not require such map-like features in your portfolio, but attention to such detail will reinforce the notion established in your Reflection Statement and revisions that you are a careful scholar who takes pride in your work.

Remember that Appearance IS Important!

Just as instructors often do not require tabs or a Table of Contents page, they often will not think to require that the portfolio be neat and attractive; they will automatically assume that you will present a polished portfolio. Do not submit an old folder (unless it is hardbound without any marks identifying that it has been used before). Unless your instructor has specific requirements, use a standard font style (for example, Courier or Times New Roman) in 10 or 12 point type with black ink. Type or print only on the front of clean, white paper (unless the course specifically lends itself to a more creative approach). In such cases, ensure that readability is not sacrificed by highly decorative paper or fonts. Be consistent with such matters on all pages.

While such recommendations may sound obvious to you, instructors frequently get portfolios that do not meet these minimum standards of professionalism or that move in the opposite direction and over-present the work. An attractive cover page gets attention and shows pride in your portfolio. However, too much emphasis on how the portfolio looks may suggest to the instructor that you are smokescreening, i.e. that your writing cannot stand on its own. The most successful portfolios strike a balance between a fresh appearance and strong writing. If you must choose between the two, opt for spending time improving your content.

Protect Your Work

If the writing you are doing relates to your major or is a Student Career Portfolio, then you will need to be sure to make photocopies or disk copies for future reference before submitting the portfolio. Even if you never plan to study this subject again, save copies or save the actual final drafts onto your hard drive or a floppy disk before you print out the instructor's copy. While instructors rarely lose student work, the possibility exists, especially at the end of a course when instructors are generally swamped with paperwork, and saving your work in such an event can prevent you from having to recreate the portfolio from memory. If the writing represents extensive primary research and a significant contribution to the topic being discussed, you might consider copyrighting the entire document. The

US Copyright Office Home Page can be found at
http://lcweb.loc.gov/copyright/. Until your work is evaluated, save all
materials from all drafts that may not have been submitted; such
evidence can provide backup support in the event the instructor
questions a source, quote, or fact.

Electronic Portfolio Submissions

Because electronic portfolios require substantially less storage
space and paper, more and more instructors and programs are
requesting electronic submission. The "...computer-based
portfolio...allows for the capture and storage of information in the form
of text, graphics, sound, and video," thus allowing students to "...save
writing samples, solutions to mathematics problems, samples of art
work, science projects, and multimedia presentations in one coherent
document" (Lankes 2). Blair and Takayoshi note how electronic
portfolios are "multilinear," "multivocal," and "multisequential" in that
they "...offer multiple paths readers might follow, depending on which
direction they choose to go" rather than merely reading straight through
a physical text (358; 357).

To prepare an electronic portfolio, start by examining the
requirements and ensuring your word processing software and
computer capabilities are compatible with your school's systems. If
they are not, then consider using school computers for submitting the
material (indeed, some schools insist that you do so); check the lab
schedule well in advance of your deadline to ensure you can fit in time
to complete the portfolio. If the material has been entered elsewhere,
but you cannot retrieve information from your floppy disk, then access
a scanner to avoid having to retype your material completely.

Electronic portfolios usually only include the final drafts of
each paper; in fact, as Tully points out, "...students don't often have
their drafts because the improvements were immediately entered on the
screen and saved as a file" (91). You should consult the assignment as
early as possible to be sure you will not need early drafts.

The web site of Kalamazoo College, located at
http://www.kzoo.edu/pfolio/pfolschools2.html, includes an accessible
database of schools that require student portfolios and offer sample
portfolios online. Examining what other students have done and are
doing can give you ideas not only about what makes for a strong

electronic portfolio but also about what you might do to make your own portfolio more technologically creative.

Submit on Disk

Once you have ensured that your system is compatible with the system that will be used to retrieve your work, discover exactly what type of disk you will need. School-compatible, pre-formatted disks are available at most college bookstores, though, occasionally, whether or not they are double or single sided can impact their usability on certain machines. Clearly mark each paper and the reflection statement by saving them onto separate files with identifying names such as "Paper One," "Report Two," "Reflection Statement," "Analysis," or "Review." You might also save an identifying file that contains your name, address, phone, email address, etc., in the event the disk gets lost or the instructor needs to contact you as he or she evaluates your portfolio. Save a copy of all of the portfolio material on both your hard drive and another floppy as backup. Clearly label your disk with your name and any other identifying material the instructor requires.

Submit via Email

Some instructors prefer that you submit your portfolio to them at their email address so they can access the work virtually anywhere without the burden of keeping up with floppies. In such cases, saving the papers as separate attachments on one email message is generally preferred rather than sending separate emails for each paper. Once again, ensure that the instructor can access information from your software; if the attachments are not accessible, you may be able to insert portfolio material directly into the email message although such message boxes frequently have limited space and may result in unorthodox margins that can disorient the reader. Save a copy of all of the portfolio material on both your hard drive and another floppy as backup.

Develop a CD-ROM Portfolio

A CD-ROM portfolio offers the portability of an email and the non-web-dependent flexibility of a floppy disk while also providing exciting opportunities for sound and graphics. Many teacher education portfolios are now on CD-ROM because videos of student teaching can so readily be included. You will need to have access to CD-ROM-producing equipment; contact your computer or technology services office to find out if or where such equipment is available on your campus.

Develop a Web Page or Hypertext Portfolio

Instructors are increasingly insisting that portfolio work be posted to a web page; in fact, actually developing the web page may be part of the assignment. If you are required to do this, you need to start early in learning not only how to construct a web page but also the most effective way to present your material. Usually, presenting each assignment within a creative click-on page is most effective. Blair and Takayoshi go one step farther with this suggestion:

> A student might start with the first draft, for example, and draw links between that writing and invention notes which influenced it, revised versions of sections of the writing, and responses by teacher and students to segments of the writing. (368)

Online portfolios as such are beginning to elevate overall the importance of appearance because they are presented through such a visual medium. Test your page online to ensure that it actually is accessible and that all of the pages work as planned. Do not, however, be so overwhelmed with the technological aspects that you neglect an emphasis on sound writing. Work also, however, to ensure that the text is visually appealing. Instructors Blair and Takayoshi warn, "...the construction of electronic portfolios requires a blend of print, pictures, and sound to achieve rhetorical effectiveness" (362).

You might consider using one of several commercially available portfolio programs for developing your on-line portfolio. Aurbach's "Grady Profile," Roger Wagner Publishing's "HyperStudio," and Claris' "FileMaker Pro" might save you time by providing templates for certain documents (see Lankes 2). Other packages are available on the Internet or, possibly, from your campus computer network.

Creating an electronic portfolio has the added advantage of serving as proof of your technological abilities in the workforce; Blair and Takayoshi suggest that such portfolios "...might function outside the classroom context as a demonstration of their [students'] design abilities and a collection of their own work for potential job interviews and employers" (361).

Protect Your Work

Aside from copying your material onto your hard drive, saving at least one electronic back-up (such as a floppy, CD-ROM, or web page), or copyrighting the work via the US Copyright Office (http://lcweb.loc.gov/copyright/), another strategy you may employ for web pages specifically is a statement at the bottom of your page revealing any uses of your material that you authorize. Because of the nature of the Internet, however, your control of any material is much more limited than hard copy, disk, or email submissions. Additional resources about electronic portfolios are listed in Appendix G.

Your Role

Find out as early as possible how the portfolio should be submitted. If it needs to be electronic, discover immediately if your home computer system is compatible with the system your instructor will be using; if it is not, use a system, such as your school's, that will work. Do not ignore the importance of appearance regardless of how it is submitted.

Preparing Your Portfolio

Which portfolio does your instructor require?

Physical
↓
What kind of folder is required?

What order of assignments is required?

What are the format and font requirements?

Is the portfolio neat?

Should you identify portfolio sections?

Do you need to include rough & final drafts?

Electronic
↓
Will the portfolio need to be submitted on disk, email, CD-ROM or web page?

What system requirements does your instructor have for accessing your work?

Is your system compatible?

If not, can you scan rather than retype?

Have you provided links between electronic documents?

Are those links clear, appropriate, and easily accessed?

Have you saved a copy?

Should you further protect your work?

Works Cited

Blair, Kristine L. and Pamela Takayoshi. "Reflections on Reading and
Evaluating Electronic Portfolios." *Situating Portfolios: Four
Perspectives.* Eds. Kathleen Blake Yancey and Irwin Weiser.
Logan, UT: Utah State UP, 1997. 357-369.

Lankes, Anna Maria D. *Electronic Portfolios: A New Idea in
Assessment.* Syracuse, NY: ERIC Digest. 1995. ED 390377.
2/1/2000.
http://www.ed.gov/databases/ERIC_Digests/ed390377.html

Romano, Tom. "Multigenre Research: One College Senior." *Portfolio
Portraits.* Eds. Donald H. Graves and Bonnie S. Sunstein.
Portsmouth, NH: Heinemann, 1992. 146-157.

Tully, Marianne. *Helping Students Revise Their Writing.* New York:
Scholastic Professional Books, 1996.

Chapter 7
Follow Up

> *"Portfolios ought to be personal documents of our personal literacy histories. Keeping a portfolio is a long and disciplined process" (Sunstein xii).*

Answer the following:

➤ What has been meaningful about the portfolio process?

➤ Did the grade your portfolio received match what you expected it would receive?

➤ What employers might want to see a copy of your portfolio?

➤ What will such a copy suggest about your writing and organizational skills?

After the portfolio is submitted, you may have the tendency to forget about it. You should not relegate it to memory, however, because it may become valuable for professional or at least sentimental reasons.

Collect Portfolio After Release Date

Often, instructors will release physical portfolios immediately after grading them. More frequently, however, they will allow you to pick up the portfolio during the next academic term (or after a certain number of years, if it is a Program Assessment Portfolio). Write down, as an end-of-the-current-year reminder that you need to pick up the portfolio as soon as possible. Then, follow through and pick it up. The instructor will probably be glad to see you as well as pleased to free up shelf space of at least one portfolio.

Request Response to the Work

After a great deal of time has elapsed, instructors may not remember the strengths of your portfolio and, because of end-of-term grading crunches, may not have responded at length to your portfolio, especially if he or she had already recommended changes to multiple drafts. Callahan notes that a variety of feedback is possible to portfolios: "When teachers evaluate portfolios, some give oral or written comments; others use a check-off sheet, referring to specific elements, a descriptive label, numbers keyed to a rubric, or a combination of responses" (119). Usually, the letter grade suffices for most students as evidence of the quality of work in the portfolio. However, if the portfolio deals with subject matter in your major, you may want to request additional feedback to help you prepare the document for future use in your career. Be aware that faculty members are often pressed for time, but a request for returning to pick up feedback and the portfolio within two to three weeks is not unreasonable.

Challenge the Portfolio Grade, If Necessary

Occasionally, students and instructors disagree on the grade a portfolio should receive. If this is the case for you, first clarify with the instructor that the grade—for the course and/or the portfolio—is correct. Professors DO make mistakes. Clarify that other factors such as attendance or participation did not affect your grade. Then, if the portfolio grade is still unsatisfactory, request a response in writing (following the above steps) concerning its faults. Sometimes, instructors' initial reactions to your writing do not reflect their conception of your overall ability at the end of the course; David Smit explains, "...the large majority of disputes over portfolios generally occurs for this reason: an instructor originally grades a paper much too quickly or carelessly and either gives the paper a passing grade or does not adequately inform the student how to improve it" (311). While this might be the case in your own paper and it is unfortunate, the grade might also be a result of your careless portfolio collection or insufficient revision and editing.

The best approach is to remain calm and rational, to state your case clearly to the instructor, and to keep copies of all of your documents and records of your meetings with the instructor. If the instructor is unwilling to discuss your plight, then ask to speak to the director of his or her program and/or the department chair. He or she should be able to point you to the university's appeal policy. If that doesn't work, contact your university's ombudsman or vice-president for student services. Know going in that the most successful appeals are those where the student has complete and accurate records of his or her work in the course. Frequently, a deadline applies to appeals; usually, it falls early within the next semester after the course was taken. Even if you appeal, the grade ultimately might not change, and you will be well-advised to remember that "...evaluating writing is often a messy, subjective, and even quarrelsome business" (Smit 312).

Apply the Process to
Professional/Academic Situations

You may find it helpful to use the portfolio when preparing to get a job in your field as an example of the kind of polished work you can produce. Generally, you can copy a physical portfolio that includes the markings and comments from the instructor. If the portfolio is on a floppy or CD-ROM, you can leave a copy with your employer, or, if it is on a web page, you can put the web address on your resume. Indeed, the skills you develop as a result of writing the portfolio can help you gather, write, and submit research for final documents in other courses or once you begin your career. As Tom Romano puts it, "When you get down to it, it's not the portfolio that matters most. The portfolio could become no more than a file, dog-eared, jammed in a desk or stored in a box high atop a cabinet. What does matter, however, is the portfolio *process*" (157).

Your Role

The portfolio promises to gain in value for you as evidence of your ability for other instructors, for potential employers, and for yourself. Keep it for future reference.

Preparing Your Portfolio

When can you retrieve the portfolio?

Where will it be stored?

Can feedback from it help you develop career materials?

Can you use it or the skills learned in it to help in other courses or jobs?

If it is electronic, how can it be updated to reflect your ongoing writing and career progress?

Works Cited

Callahan, Susan. "Portfolio Expectations: Possibilities and Limits."
Assessing Writing 2.2 (1995): 117-151.

Romano, Tom. "Multigenre Research: One College Senior." *Portfolio Portraits*. Eds. Donald H. Graves and Bonnie S. Sunstein. Portsmouth, NH: Heinemann, 1992. 146-157.

Smit, David W. "A WPA's Nightmare: Reflections on Using Portfolios as a Course Exit Exam." *New Directions in Portfolio Assessment: Reflective Practice, Critical Theory, and Large-Scale Scoring*. Eds. Laurel Black, Donald Daiker, Jeffrey Sommers, and Gail Stygall. Portsmouth, NH: Boynton/Cook, 1994. 303-313.

Sunstein, Bonnie. S. "Introduction." *Portfolio Portraits*. Eds. Donald H. Graves and Bonnie S. Sunstein. Portsmouth, NH: Heinemann, 1992. xi-xvii.

Sweet, David. "Student Portfolios: Classroom Uses." Education Research CONSUMER GUIDE No. 8, Nov. 1993. Office of Educational Research and Improvement, US Department of Education. 2/1/2000.
http://www.ed.gov/pubs/OR/ConsumerGuides/classuse.html

Appendix A
Glossary

Electronic Portfolio—a portfolio submitted via email, web page, floppy disk, or other electronic medium.

Final Portfolio—a portfolio that demonstrates your ultimate writing skills in the class. It highlights your best work on the required number of assignments.

Global Revision—the process of revising for overall changes before doing sentence-level editing.

Growth Portfolio—a portfolio that shows the evaluator your development as a writer. It may include every draft of one particular essay, what you consider to be your worst or best draft and why, or drafts from various stages in the course.

Individual Course Portfolio—a portfolio designed to assess your performance in one class only. It can be a final portfolio or a growth portfolio.

Merged Portfolio—a portfolio that combines elements of the growth portfolio and the final portfolio.

Physical Portfolio—a portfolio that is submitted in hard copy, usually collected in a particular type of folder.

Program Administrator—the evaluator beyond your instructor who assesses program assessment portfolios.

Program Assessment Portfolio—a portfolio that is designed to assess how well students are learning in courses or in a program. It may or may not count toward course credit. It can be either a final or growth portfolio; most are final portfolios.

Reflection Statement—introduces the portfolio. Serves a major role in determining the personality of the portfolio and establishing how well you have absorbed the lessons learned in the course.

Revision—the process of re-seeing your work from multiple angles. More than just editing, it incorporates developing and re-organizing your ideas.

Student Career Portfolio—a portfolio that is designed to represent a student's academic career, whether for the student's entire time at a college or university or for certain programs within the university, such as general education requirements. It can be either a final or growth portfolio.

Appendix B
Teacher Education Portfolios

Portfolios for students in teacher education programs have unique characteristics and thus deserve special mention. The purpose of such portfolios is to demonstrate graduating seniors' abilities to enter a teaching career. The portfolios may be either growth (or "formative") or final (sometimes called "eligibility" portfolios). All teacher education portfolios share some common elements. For instance, the Kentucky New Teacher Standards require all graduating education majors in that state to submit portfolios that prove the future teachers are able to design and plan instruction, to create a learning-based classroom, and to assess instruction, among other things. Such goals can be achieved by including some of the following:

- Lesson or unit plan

- Videotape that documents teaching ability

- Personal narrative reflecting on teaching or on an observation

- Philosophy of teaching

- Assessment measures and scoring guides or rubrics, etc. (Murray State University)

Campbell et al. provide an entire chapter and a checklist about artifacts that might be included in the portfolio. Edgerton, Hutchings, and Quinlan provide an exhaustive list of "Possible items for inclusion" which suggests that teacher education students need to include descriptive material from themselves as well as from others, including their students and their colleagues (8). They also stress the importance of combining documentation with insight: "...work samples plus reflection make a powerful formula" (Edgerton, Hutchings, and Quinlan 9). Robert Yagelski likewise emphasizes the need for teacher education portfolios to be "critically reflective" and to demonstrate the pre-teachers' potential for continuing reflection about their teaching (233).

Most teacher education portfolios are Program Assessment portfolios, although many teacher education programs include several individual courses that also have portfolio components. For instance, Carol Osborne's graduate course in Teaching Literature to Adolescents at Murray State University requires a portfolio that includes 8 of 10 assignments, a unit lesson plan, and a teaching philosophy statement. The teaching statement will, more than likely, be included in a Program Assessment Portfolio as well. Dr. Osborne asks students to prove their "knowledge of adolescent literature" as well as their teaching abilities.

Students who are compiling a teacher education portfolio should be sure to consult their major departments, their university education department and, if necessary, their state department of education to ensure they have complete information about what is required of the teacher education portfolio, who will be the audience for it, what type of portfolio it is designed to be, and when it is due. The information in the rest of this text is applicable for teacher education portfolios, and additional teacher education portfolio resources can be found in Appendix G.

Works Cited

Campbell, Dorothy M., et al. *How to Develop a Professional Portfolio: A Manual for Teachers*. Boston: Allyn & Bacon, 1997.

Edgerton, Russell, Patricia Hutchings, and Kathleen Quinlan. *The Teaching Portfolio: Capturing the Scholarship in Teaching*. The AAHE Teaching Initiative of the American Association for Higher Education. 1991.

Murray State University Department of Elementary and Secondary Education. *Portfolios in Teacher Education*. 1999.

Osborne, Carol. "Your Professional Portfolio." ENG 529. Fall1999 Syllabus. Murray, KY: Murray State University.

Yagelski, Robert P. "Portfolios as a Way to Encourage Reflective Practice among Preservice English Teachers." *Situating Portfolios: Four Perspectives*. Eds. Kathleen Blake Yancey and Irwin Weiser. Logan, UT: Utah State UP, 1997. 225-243.

Appendix C
Unsuccessful Reflection Statements

Student 1

This student does not explain the concrete portfolio revisions made to each paper nor the specific changes made within the student's overall writing. Too much attention is given to pre-course events and too little to what happened during the semester.

Dr. Claywell,

In my portfolio are three pieces I have worked on this semester. I came into the class in August with a history of good writing. I had some excellent teachers in middle school and high school who worked with me to perfect my writing. What I've always been good at is writing my words as I would speak them. My teachers helped me develop my creativity, saying "show, not tell." This class added more depth to my writing by teaching me how to give it maturity and credibility. I've learned how to read someone else's work and analyze it more thoroughly, going beyond what the author is saying, and asking why the author is saying it, and to whom, and why it is important.

My favorite piece in this portfolio is the first piece, "To Believe or Not To Believe: The Grounds for Religious Faith." I like it because I believe I learned something as I wrote it. I'm always more proud of my writing when I enjoy writing it, especially when I learn from it. I believe this entire portfolio demonstrates my growth as a writer, and I hope you enjoy reading it as much as I enjoyed writing it.

Very Sincerely
Student 1

Student 2

This student offers some specific changes made to each paper, but the analysis of the student's growth as a writer is too skimpy and detached. The final paragraph moves toward trying to appease at the risk of alienating the teacher. The statement also needs careful editing.

Student 2
Dr. Claywell
12.07.99

Reflection Paper

My portfolio includes three essays which were rather average as show by my grade. All three needed both grammatical work as well as more expansion and clarity.

In the first paper, "Apples or Oranges", I went back and add more ideas, as well as move some ideas around to help the paper read easier. I also fixed the grammatical errors as well as put it in MLA.

In the second paper,"The Kennedy Show", I went through and changed some of my ideas in order to show how the author brought his point across rather than what his point was. So instead of it being a summary, it was an analysis. I also fixed the grammatical errors.

And the last paper, "How Figures Figure In", the main problem seemed to be the grammatical errors. I also missed a few key ideas about the authors that might influence their writing. I believe I fixed most of what was needed.

Student 3

Although this student exhibits audience awareness (and perhaps an understanding that other instructors might read it), it merely summarizes the individual papers without revealing the revisions made to them. The discussion of writing growth is too general.

Dear Reviewer,

Throughout this semester, I have written a few papers that you are about to read. In these papers you can tell there is a big difference in the style of the writings themselves. The first paper you will read is a narrative paper entitled "Burger King." It is about the many aspirations of teenagers and violence. The second paper is entitled, "Are Biracials treated fairly in today's society?" It is a rhetorical analysis about a young biracial mans essay. The third and final paper you will read is entitled, "Generation-X." As you can tell this is about today's youth in society. This paper is a contextual analysis over three essays I have read in class. I chose to write this paper because we Gen.-X are always being labeled as a lower class than our predecessors the "Baby Boomers."

As you can tell my writing did improve over each of the three essays. My best probably being the last one I had written. My first paper I wrote sounds like a high school writing, but my last is college level in my view. I hope that you enjoy these papers you are about to read, and thank you for the time you are about take in readings these papers.

Sincerely

Student 3

Appendix D
Good Reflection Statements

Student 4

This student identifies the general writing improvements made throughout the course. Then, the student discusses at length the changes made to each paper. The student reveals an understanding of the concepts taught in the course applicable to the writing

Reflection Statement

Throughout the course of my first year in college, I think my writing has improved substantially. I have always enjoyed writing, and I usually use proper grammar, mechanics, punctuation, etc. However, this year I have learned to write more effectively using sophisticated sentences and active voice, yet also being concise in my thoughts and ideas. I have also learned many argumentative strategies that are resourceful when trying to persuade audiences. I noticed an improvement in each of my writings as the semester passed, learning to write more professionally and still appeal to the reader.

My first paper, a reflective argument about LBL, had very few mechanical errors. Only a small number of structural changes were required, so I had to revise it once more and make the necessary adjustments. Mainly, I needed to tighten some of my ideas and state my point in a more succinct manner. For example, I used prepositional phrases and some other words that were superfluous and had to be condensed. I also got rid of a nominalization by changing the noun, formation, back into a verb.

My second paper was a research report in which I stated and analyzed the results of a survey I conducted. Like my first paper, this one didn't have many grammatical errors, but it did have a few organizational problems. To correct these, I moved a couple of sentences around so that each

Student 4 (Continued)

in the portfolio. The student forecasts the strategies necessary for future writing improvement. Finally, the paper is well-written and carefully edited.

sentence in every paragraph was related to the topic sentence of that paragraph. As always, there were some words that I changed and omitted in order to make sentences sound better and more suitable.

My last paper, a rhetorical analysis detailing the effects of alcohol in inner cities, had some minor errors that needed to be corrected. I had to clarify a few points and rearrange a sentence so that it could be understood better. Mainly, I changed several "be" verbs to action verbs and eliminated as many passive sentences as possible. This helped to make the paper more interesting and concise.

I have noticed several improvements in my writings as I progressed throughout the semester. I have tried to write using as many active verbs as possible and do away with needless words and phrases. To make my writings sound more professional, I have also tried to cut down on short, choppy sentences and write more elaborate, sophisticated sentences. However, I still attempt to organize my ideas so that they are condensed and logical to the reader. I learned to use the three persuasive strategies: logos, ethos, and pathos. These are very important when trying to convince and influence others, and I will always try to use them when they are needed. I now know that writing can be a very effective means of communication, and when done correctly, it can be even better than speaking. If I continue to work on these areas of my writing, especially sentence structure and organization, I think I can become a good, maybe even great, writer as I continue on in college and the rest of my life.

Student 5

This student (a marketing major) displays personality and voice in this statement. From this angle alone, it makes pleasurable reading. However, the student also discusses the specific changes made to each paper, assessing both the strengths and weaknesses

Student 5
8 December 1999
English 101-10
Dr. Claywell

You are preparing to embark on an adventure through endless pages of my ramblings—a pile constructed of random thoughts, masked confusion, and intellectual inspirations. This is an end result of a semester bombarded by massive amounts of writings; however, a fulfilling moment that it is completed. Each paper in the collection is unique and has different strengths of its own.

My first concoction is entitled "The Essence of Time," a narrative depicting my view on how time affects society—both good and bad. The strength to it is that I was able to reflect on some moments in my past that have enlightened me to the hold that time has. Weaknesses are that I used sentence fragments often and may not have foreshadowed where I was going with the piece. "Wanted: Heroes" has the same predicament, not enough foreshadowing, but it is difficult to indicate what is going to happen when one is doing an analysis. However, I enjoyed constructing this piece because it exposed some aspects to heroism that I had taken for granted and did not know. My third piece, "Barbie: Continuing Controversy" takes on an underlying feministic tone that tells of how Barbie was constructed and how different authors perceive the aging doll. This contextual analysis depicts three different writer's works, and how each easily explained herself. My final selection was a humor piece to me, yet I must admit that I do not feel that my best was done on it.

Student 5 (Continued)

of each. The student might have devoted more attention to the analysis of overall writing development. While the student reveals an understanding of the importance of audience awareness, the final paragraph might be construed as overly personable, even pushy.

"Crest is the Best" was written as a persuasive essay eager to appeal consumers to the enticement of the toothpaste, Crest. However, when I got into the depths of research, the figures I needed to back certain points up were unavailable, therefore putting a stint in my writing aptitude.

Overall, my experience in English 101 has been pleasant, enjoyable, yet stressful at moments. I believe that I have advanced in the way I am able to express my ways through writing, and I have learned that procrastination is not the best thing to do. Since I did procrastinate this semester, I learned a valuable lesson: Procrastination equals stress equals not so good paper equals eventually fail English 101 equals repeat next semester with me in your class again. So, please pass me. That would be for the best. Thank you in advance for your willingness to adhere to my wishes. In all seriousness, I hope that you are not bored in the least with this portfolio, and while you have found this letter a tad whimsical, I hope it remains relevant.

Student 6

This student understands what needs improvement. Ironically, one weakness appears not to have been overcome—careful editing. This statement does reveal, however, the student's understanding of the need to adapt writing to the audience and purpose. The paper discusses,

---

Student 6
08 December 1999
Dr. G. Claywell
English 101-10

Reflection Statement

In high school I was terrified of writing papers. I had a hard time expressing my ideas and making my writing flow. I never though my writing would be good enough. So sitting in English 101 the first day of college, I was timid and scared. After all, this was a college course that required a different level of writing--different from the typical book reports and movie reviews that I had completed in high school. For my first college English assignment, I had no idea on where to begin. However, I slowly began conquer my fear of writing. I spent a great deal of time writing and reviewing all of the assigned papers. Not only did I want to excel in my writing, but I also wanted to build confidence in my writing skills.

Before taking English 101 during the fall of 1999, my writing withheld many weaknesses. My sentences were choppy and my ideas did not flow well. I rarely used transitional words, but I often used too many prepositional phrases. Above all, though, careless mistakes in spelling and grammar plagued my writing. Recognizing these faults gave me a goal to strive for--turning my weaknesses into strengths. My writing reflects a part of me and how I make decisions. If I want to be brief and to the point I tend to use short sentences. If I want to explain in detail an idea I am trying to get across, I use longer sentences, commas, and semi-colons to tie in my writing. My writing can be personal, formal, or informal. That's what's great about writing. Generally, I can write as freely as I wish to and make my own decisions. I have

Student 6 (Continued)

although briefly, the changes made to the papers and future changes that need to be made to improve the student's writing. The writing is personable and seems sincere.

learned a lot about myself by writing. I have learned that I am not an effective procrastinator. I like to have plenty of time to make my writing the best it can be. I have also learned not to underestimate my ability. I might not be the best writer, but if I have a positive attitude, things usually turn out well. Finally, I have learned the power of commas and transitional words: they really do make sentences flow better.

Much of my transformation can be attributed to Dr. Claywell. She introduced me to the MLA format. After writing four papers, I am now comfortable with this style. Her advice has proven helpful; she has helped me understand and correct the mistakes I have made. Handouts are another useful tool Dr. Claywell has provided. If I have questions then I am able to refer to these sheets.

In my narrative paper I was able to take my imagination and run with it. I also was able to intertwine my imagination and reality. One thing I noticed in this particular paper was the constant use of all the "be" verbs. My writing could sound stronger if I make the nouns of the sentences actual "doers" of the action. In the rhetorical analysis, I made several careless mistakes. At first I sounded repetitive on some of the material. Finally, in the contextual analysis, I gravitated toward making short, choppy sentences. Correcting these papers helped me realize what areas of writing I need to be aware of when finalizing a paper.

Goals for English 102 are to continue overcome my weaknesses. Though I am conscious about the mistakes and have improved greatly, I still have a long way to go in writing. I would like to be able to revise my own papers effectively. In future papers I am going to use more parallelism. My overall growth has been tremendous.

Appendix E
Better Reflection Statements

Student 7

This student reflects an awareness that the course and the portfolio must merge the ideas important to the professor or program with the student's development as a writer and scholar. The tone of this statement is personal

---

Student 7
Dr. Claywell
Eng 104-01
30 April 1999

Time to Reflect

Before our English 104 class met for the first time, the professor had goals for us. She designed the class to "help students improve their writing, research, and argumentative skills...develop stronger critical thinking skills, contextual awareness, and organizational effectiveness." I suppose that I had many of the same goals for my own writing but simply thought of it as "making my writing sound better." In addition, I wanted to gain confidence in my writing. Before this class, I felt as though my writing was inferior to others and unworthy of submission in an honors composition class.

This class has boosted the confidence I have in my writing by improving some simple errors that appeared quite often in my work. Within this portfolio, I have included the main projects from this class to show the improvements that I made in my writing as the semester progressed. Each assignment of this semester taught me about a new technique or a stylistic problem that affected my work.

The first assignment required research, argumentative techniques, and organization in the form of a reflective argument. This assignment helped me acquire better research skills and organizational skills while getting me back

Student 7 (Continued)

yet academic. The student discusses at great lengths the specific changes made to the final drafts.

in the habit of writing. The rusty draft that I handed in needed many grammatical corrections as well as clearer wording. I added a hint of forecasting in the introduction to introduce the organizational layout of the paper. I also reworded a large part of the conclusion to reduce repetitiveness. After editing this paper for a second time, I realized how far my writing has come in the last semester.

The second assignment, a research report, contained elements that I had never practiced in previous classes. Creating a survey that asked the questions that I wanted answered and reporting the results in an objective report seemed quite elementary. However, the task became a struggle when I could not fit all the questions I had for the surveyed group into a concise questionnaire. In addition, I wanted to include my opinion within the results, which the assignment did not allow, Specific stylistic problems appeared in this assignment, such as using "be" verbs, passive voice, and paragraphs lacking coherence and cohesion. I corrected these problems by changing several "be" verbs into action verbs and reorganizing paragraphs so that the focus of each paragraph became more apparent. I also reworded several sentences to improve the flow of the paragraphs and paper as a whole. Finally, at the advice of my teacher, I added a sentence about advertising mentor programs to the conclusion, which I had removed from the rough draft. The third major writing assignment posed a new challenge for me. I was very unfamiliar with the concept of rhetorical analysis and had to learn what such a paper contained. After I wrote and submitted the paper, I had to make a few minor grammatical and typographical corrections. I added a sentence to the introduction to entice readers before leaping into the

Student 7 (Continued)

Each paper gets a full paragraph's description, and the student includes both content and usage revisions. The

discussion of the analyzed article. Within the body of the paper, I added the explanation of the author's use of second person to address the readers directly. This fit well with my previous discussion of his use of third person within the article. Again, I changed the wording of several sentences to reduce confusion and unnecessary complexity.

The next paper within the portfolio illustrates the ideas I had for the largest assignment, the argumentative research paper. This research proposal offers an audience analysis as well as a "plan of attack" for the paper. I included this paper in the portfolio to represent the effort that went into the most significant project of the semester. While it is not the actual research paper, it reveals the main purpose of the argumentative assignment, including why I chose the topic of mentoring and how I conducted research for the project.

The last selection included in the portfolio exhibits the in-class work that helped shape my final research paper. The in-class pieces forced me to think quickly and thoroughly while applying lessons from the textbook to my own writing. The prompt questions that the teacher chose helped me think critically about what problems existed in my paper in addition to ways to remedy the problems. My paper would have contained biased, disputable primary sources and arguments without the aid of the in-class writing assignments.

My writing has changed drastically during the course of this class. I have become conscious of my tendency to use passive voice and "be" verbs and am developing a writing style that includes active verbs. I now write paragraphs that have more focus, keeping cohesion and coherence in mind so that I do not lose the readers' attention and comprehension. Throughout the semester, I learned many pointers for

Student 7 (Continued)

student admits the areas of the course that were new—such as the survey that served as a new learning experience.

evaluating sources within my own research and the reports of others. Most importantly, I have become much more confident in my writing ability.

While focusing on these lessons, I would like to continue improving my style of writing, concentrating on active verb usage and cohesion/coherence. I would also like to continue making my writing more clear and understandable. I tend to use unusual sounding phrases that, if simplified, would improve the readability of my work. Most of all, I want to always write with a clear purpose, smooth transitions, and powerful conclusions that leave the reader with a simple "WOW!"

Student 8

This reflection statement points to specific knowledge gained in the course. The student clearly explains what weaknesses were apparent in the initial drafts as well as the changes made to improve or remove

Student 8
Dr. Claywell
Eng. Comp. 102-05
7 December 1998

My Reflection of Composition

In the past few months of work in English Composition many important topics have been covered. With the various writing exercises and readings I have learned much about how to compose debates, respond to arguments, and analyze other arguments. With this newfound knowledge I have also noticed an improvement in my writing style and techniques. This is evident in the portfolio's three essays, which I will later point out. Overall, my writing skills have improved.

While reading the arguments and other essays assigned, one of the things I learned includes the way in which different strategies are used to make an affective argument. Among these are the different organizations of arguments like the Rogerian Argument and the Toulmin Model argument. Another aspect of arguments that I have learned is how to more easily recognize when fallacies are used. This is helpful when debating any subject in which the opponent is trying to prove something where there are no facts to back his claim. One more important part of writing that I have improved upon is obtaining the information needed to back up ones point. This skill can be helpful when writing an argumentative paper or nearly any other type of writing that requires outside sources.

Student 8 (Continued)

those weaknesses. More significantly, the student reveals an understanding of the different layers on which writing operates: grammar improvement is necessary, but the writer sees "the most important improvements" as being

---

The improvements made in my writing over the last few months are evident in the portfolio. With the first piece, "The Basis of Christian Faith", there was a slight problem with grammar and a little more of a problem with disorganization. After the revisions the majority of the grammar problems were corrected and the organization was improved. The grammar was improved by adding commas and other punctuation where needed and changing words to better fit the sentence structures. The other problem areas such as organization were fixed by moving certain sentences from one paragraph to another, by deleting some completely, and adding others where needed to fit the assignment.

The second piece of writing which I have revised, "Animal Rights", had mainly grammar problems, and a few left out sentences. The technical problems were mainly due to the use of too many extra words and an incorrect page layout. The few sentences added helped strengthen the points of the essay and tie together some of the more distantly related subjects.

The final essay, "An Analysis of TV Violence Arguments", had more grammatical errors, but was better organized and thought out. Its main problem was the lack of an effective opening and closing paragraph. This was corrected again by adding and combining certain sentences to improve the flow and support for the body of the essay. Along with these corrections, a few common grammar problems were solved and a few of the more wordy phrases were removed.

Overall, I believe the biggest improvement in the area of grammar that can be shown with the three essays is the better use of punctuation and wording. I would say the most

Student 8 (Continued)

a stronger argumentative awareness—thus revealing the
student's increased writing and cognitive maturity.

important improvements are those in the analysis of
arguments which help one to react to the opposition better and
which help tremendously when writing papers such as the
final essay in this portfolio.

Appendix F
Successful Portfolio Revisions

Student 9

This student admits that this particular paper was a
difficult choice to include (this particular class had to
choose 3 of 6 papers for the portfolio). The author
understands the significance of being changed by the

Excerpt from Reflection Statement of Student 9:

Choosing the last paper to revise was a bit tougher. The first
two that I revised were the two that I knew the most about, so
I found it much easier to add information and opinions to
them. The paper on school uniforms was the final one that I
chose. I haven't had any personal experience with school
uniforms, so I didn't have as many opinions to add. This paper
was, however, interesting for me to write. As I said in my
strategy, I started writing it to tell people why students should
not be forced to wear uniforms to school, but through my
research I changed my opinion about school uniforms. A
paper makes a dramatic impact on the author when the
author's views are actually changed during the course of
writing it. When revising this paper, I mainly looked at my
word choice and use of "be" verbs. With this paper, I also
looked at the actors as the subjects of sentences. Although I
didn't add as much to this paper, it reads more smoothly after
the revision.

Student 9 (Continued)

research and writing of a paper; the student's knowledge
and attitude about the topic changed totally in the writing of
the paper. Such a reversal suggests to the teacher that the

First Draft, Student 9:

Student 9
ENG 404
Paper #3
9/27/99

Purpose: To report
Audience: Parents of children in public schools
Topic: School uniforms
Format: Essay
Strategy: When I started to write this paper, I was going to
write about why students should not be forced to wear
uniforms. However, after reading the articles I saw that school
uniforms aren't such a bad idea. I chose to discuss the
advantages of school uniforms starting by what they can do
for students, then for parents. I purposely saved reducing
violence for the end. So much attention is focused on violence
in the schools these days. Although I am aware that violence
is a big issue, I want my readers to realize that there are other
problems that school uniforms can also address. I wanted this
topic at the end so that the reader would not expect the paper
to be entirely about how school uniforms can reduce violence
in the school.

Student 9 (Continued)

student has benefited from the process of writing the paper and/or being in the course. It is the ultimate evidence that the class has been worthwhile. The first draft of this paper

---

Student 9
Dr. Claywell
English 404
27 September 1999

Trouble in Our Public Schools:
Could School Uniforms Be the Answer?

Many students in school today feel like they don't belong or don't fit into the popular crowd. This is evident from the stories we hear on the news much too often. These feelings can be the cause of problems from low self-esteem to poor academic performance, even to violence in the school. Could school uniforms be the answer? Many educators and parents believe so. One is Valerie Marchant who says that with a change in dress "students may become more self-confident and self-disciplined, less judgmental of other students, better able to resist peer pressure and concentrate on schoolwork" (16). Peter Caruso agrees, saying that school uniforms increase student attendance, decrease clothing costs, improve classroom behavior, and increase academic performance (84-86).

Schools usually work with parents to decide on a particular uniform. When they picture a school uniform, most people think of the traditional Catholic uniforms, white shirts with plaid skirts for the girls or navy pants for the boys. However, uniforms can be something as simple as requiring khaki or navy pants and a particular color and style of shirt.

Students' self-esteem and self-confidence can improve by enforcing a school uniform policy. This is because many students develop feelings of inferiority when they

Student 9 (Continued)

needed improvements in organization and to avoid sentence choppiness. This version includes shifts to second person

feel they aren't wearing the "right" clothes (Caruso 84). These feelings start early. Surely most of you know students as young as third grade, maybe even first or second, who ask for Tommy Hilfiger clothes, Nike shoes, and such. Students often make fun of peers whose parents can't afford to buy the name-brand clothes each school year.

Wearing school uniforms can build self-confidence by giving students a feeling of belonging within the school. "Experts in psychology generally agree that clothing and appearance influence individual and group behavior. . . . A uniform can build the same feeling of unity and belonging that many students get from team uniforms, cheerleading outfits, or school jackets" (Caruso 85).

Attendance and academic performance also improve as a result of school uniforms. Studies show that students attend school more frequently and concentrate more on their education rather than social arrangement when they attend schools with uniform policies. Their academic performance improves as a result (Caruso 86).

Parents in school systems with uniform policies enjoy the fact that their clothing costs for their school children decrease when school uniforms are worn. After a style is decided upon, schools can order in bulk to cut parents' costs. Some schools charge slightly more to make a small profit. They devote the proceeds to students who cannot afford the uniforms. Sometimes peer pressure causes students to spend large amounts of money on school clothes. School uniforms eliminate this. Uniforms also carry over to the next school year, provided they fit, or they are passed down to younger siblings (Caruso 85). Jo Beth McDaniel interviewed some parents who have children in schools with school uniform

Student 9 (Continued)

and a lack of transitions between elements.

policies. Kim Habig, mother of three school age children, was opposed to school uniforms when the policy was first introduced. She has since changed her mind about the uniforms. Her school-clothing budget dropped by two-thirds the year after her children started wearing school uniforms (81). Another advantage of school uniforms is a decrease in school violence. You can't read about school uniforms without reading about the Long Beach Unified School District. It was the first public school system in the United States to require students to wear uniforms. In their first year with uniforms, suspensions dropped 32 percent and crime fell 36 percent (McDaniel 82). Recent studies show that these percents keep climbing. To date, criminal incidents at Long Beach schools have dropped by 86 percent since the uniforms were mandated in 1994 (Marchant 6).

Uniforms decrease violence by reducing potentially dangerous situations. "Unsuspecting children who wear gang colors or gang-related attire might be threatened or intimidated by members of opposing gangs, for example, or children who wear expensive or fashionable clothes might become victims of theft, sometimes by other students" (Paliokas, Futrell, and Rist 32). Peter Caruso says that students have been seriously injured, or even killed by students who covet what they are wearing. Competition over appearance can result in taunts, fights, thefts, and even murder (86).

Any school can see payoffs when school uniforms are mandated. "Although school uniforms do not represent a panacea for all society's problems, research shows that school uniforms do significantly affect student perceptions of school climate" (Murray 110). Jo Beth McDaniel sums it up well

Student 9 (Continued)

when she says, 'We have an entire generation of children who have grown up with no boundaries. Look what happens when you provide a few" (82).

Works Cited

Caruso, Peter. "Individuality vs. Conformity: NASSP Bulletin
    80.581 (Sept. 1996): The Issue Behind School
    Uniforms." 83-88.
Futrell, Mary Hatwood, Paliokas, Kathleen L., and Rist, Ray
    C. "Trying Uniforms On For Size." The American
    School Board Journal 183.5 (May 1996): 32-35.
Marchant, Valerie. "Dress for Success: It Looks as if
    Uniforms and Dress Codes May Well Make a
    Difference." Time 13 Sept. 1999: 6+.
McDaniel, Jo Beth. "Can Uniforms Save Our Schools?"
    Reader's Digest Sept. 1996: 79-82.

Student 9 (Continued)

This instructor's comments, coded to areas within the first draft, recommend a return to considering at least some of the negatives that the student was originally

---

Instructor's Comments to Student 9's Paper:

1. Try combining these sentences to help avoid the "be" verb in "This is."
2. This paragraph seems out of place... I recommend putting it where I have the 2nd two.
3. Who are the actors here?
4. Provide a better transition here than "Sometimes" because you're shifting away to a time when students don't have to wear uniforms.
5. Why shift to 2nd person?
6. What about the psychological effect on students who can't afford the expensive stuff!?!
7. Double space EVERYTHING in MLA!

I think you were smart to defer the violence issue. You might want to address negatives that might occur (I've heard some—mostly parents—complain that it takes away students right to express themselves creatively with their clothing. I admit it's weak, but you might think about other perspectives too). Overall, this is smoothly written. Nice job.

Student 9 (Continued)

considering to provide a balanced look at the issue. The student incorporated the instructor's comments in the revision, most noticeably in the reorganization of

---

Revised Paper, Student 9:

Student 9
Dr. Claywell
English 404
8 December 1999

Trouble in Our Public Schools:
Could School Uniforms Be the Answer?

Many students in school today feel like they don't belong or don't fit into the popular crowd. This is evident from the stories we hear on the news much too often. These feelings can cause problems that range from low self-esteem to poor academic performance, even to violence in the school. Could school uniforms be the answer? Many educators and parents believe so. One is Valerie Marchant who says that with a change in dress "students may become more self-confident and self-disciplined, less judgmental of other students, better able to resist peer pressure and concentrate on schoolwork" (16). Peter Caruso agrees, saying that school uniforms increase student attendance, decrease clothing costs, improve classroom behavior, and increase academic performance (84-86).

Since many students develop feelings of inferiority when they feel they aren't wearing the "right" clothes, their self-esteem and self-confidence can improve by enforcing a school uniform policy (Caruso 84). These feelings of inferiority start early. Surely most of you know students as young as third grade, maybe even first or second, who ask for Tommy Hilfiger clothes, Nike shoes, and such. Students often

---

Student 9 (Continued)

paragraphs early in the paper. The paper has been expanded, as well, to turn an already solid paper into

make fun of peers whose parents can't afford to buy the name-brand clothes each school year.

Wearing school uniforms can build self-confidence by giving students a feeling of belonging within the school. "Experts in psychology generally agree that clothing and appearance influence individual and group behavior. . . . A uniform can build the same feeling of unity and belonging that many students get from team uniforms, cheerleading outfits, or school jackets" (Caruso 85).

Attendance and academic performance also improve as a result of school uniforms. Studies show that students attend school more frequently and concentrate more on their education rather than social arrangement when they attend schools with uniform policies. Thus academic performance improves as a result (Caruso 86).

Parents in school systems with uniform policies enjoy the fact that their clothing costs for their school children decrease when school uniforms are worn. Schools usually work with parents to decide on a particular uniform. When most people picture a school uniform, they think of the traditional Catholic uniforms, white shirts with plaid skirts for the girls and navy pants for the boys. However, uniforms can be as simple as requiring khaki or navy pants and a particular color and style of shirt. After administrators and parents decide upon a style, schools can order in bulk to cut parents' costs. Some schools charge slightly more to make a small profit. They devote the proceeds to students who cannot afford the uniforms.

Peer pressure can cause students to spend large amounts of money on school clothes. School uniforms eliminate this. Uniforms also carry over to the next school

Student 9 (Continued)

an even better one. On this page, she acknowledges some
of the arguments that might have fueled her initial feelings

year, provided they fit, or they are passed down to younger
siblings (Caruso *85)*. Jo Beth McDaniel interviewed some
parents who have children in schools with school uniform
policies. Kim Habig, mother of three school age children, was
opposed to school uniforms when the policy was first
introduced. She has since changed her mind about the
uniforms. Her school-clothing budget dropped by two-thirds
the year after her children started wearing school uniforms
(81).

Another advantage of school uniforms is a decrease
in school violence. Long Beach Unified School District was
the first public school system in the United States to require
students to wear uniforms. In their first year with uniforms,
suspensions dropped 32 percent and crime fell 36 percent
(McDaniel 82). Recent studies show that these percents keep
climbing. To date, criminal incidents at Long Beach schools
have dropped by 86 percent since the uniforms were mandated
in 1994 (Marchant 6).

Uniforms decrease violence by reducing potentially
dangerous situations. "Unsuspecting children who wear gang
colors or gang-related attire might be threatened or
intimidated by members of opposing gangs, for example, or
children who wear expensive or fashionable clothes might
become victims of theft, sometimes by other students"
(Paliokas, Futrell, and Rist 32). Peter Caruso says that
students have been seriously injured, or even killed, by
students who covet what they are wearing. Competition over
appearance can result in taunts, fights, thefts, and even murder
(86).

Some parents may argue that mandating a school
uniform policy takes away students' rights to express

Student 9 (Continued)

about school uniforms. The student discusses the issue briefly, putting aside any concerns about student expression, and then moves on. By doing so, the student at least admits a willingness to look at all sides.

themselves. By mandating school uniforms, students will find alternative, more positive, ways to express themselves. Parents in school districts with school uniform policies have found this to be true. Most parents who were at first opposed to school uniforms changed their minds when they saw the benefits of their children wearing school uniforms.

Any school can see payoffs when school uniforms are mandated. "Although school uniforms do not represent a panacea for all society's problems, research shows that school uniforms do significantly affect student perceptions of school climate" (Murray 110). Jo Beth McDaniel sums it up well when she says, 'We have an entire generation of children who have grown up with no boundaries. Look what happens when you provide a few" (82).

Works Cited

Caruso, Peter. "Individuality vs. Conformity: The Issue Behind School Uniforms." NASSP Bulletin 80.581 (Sept. 1996): 83-88.

Futrell, Mary Hatwood, Paliokas, Kathleen L., and Rist, Ray C. "Trying Uniforms On For Size." The American School Board Journal 183.5 (May 1996): 32-35.

Marchant, Valerie. 'Dress for Success: It Looks as if Uniforms and Dress Codes May Well Make a Difference." Time 13 Sept. 1999: 6+.

McDaniel, Jo Beth. "Can Uniforms Save Our Schools?" Reader's Digest Sept. 1996: 79-82.

Student 10

This student's long introductory paragraph is followed by several short, newspaper-column-length ones. The instructor encouraged the student to start

First Draft, Student 10:
Professor Claywell
English 104-0 1
8 February 1999

Promises

When President John F. Kennedy included the Tennessee Valley Authority (TVA) in his vision of a "great nationwide land reclamation project" in 1963, his purpose was two-fold (Concept Zero). His idea was to create a recreational area that would stay as close to "wilderness condition" as possible, while attracting visitors enough to stimulate the regional economy with tourism capital (ConceptZero). The area in Western Kentucky and Tennessee, originally referred to as "Between the Rivers," was to be made available for low-impact recreational activities, such as "fishing, hunting, hiking, camping, boating, and environmental education" (Concept Zero). There was one outstanding problem, however, in the President's plan for what would later come to be known as "Land Between the Lakes" (LBL). This property happened to be owned by private citizens, many of whom had ties to the land dating as far back as the Revolutionary War, and they were not thrilled with the idea of selling (Concept Zero).

Obviously something caused the residents of the land to leave since LBL is now the 179,000 acre protected home of approximately 1300 plant species, 600 animal and bird species, and 76 species of fish (Concept Zero). But what was it? Or, better yet, who was it?

When the families in the Kentucky/Tennessee region refused to move, TVA gave them no choice - they invoked "eminent domain" and practically stole the land from the

Student 10 (Continued)

experimenting with longer, more-developed paragraphs
more representative of an academic style.   The student's

remaining residents (Concept Zero) But to smooth over the
situation, TVA representatives made many verbal promises to
the LBL refugees, keeping in line with the mission that
Kennedy set out to achieve (Concept Zero). Among these
assurances were: "unimpeded access. . . to the numerous small
cemeteries, no commercial development within the LBL
lands, no occupied dwellings to remain or be built on LBL
lands, and no private inholdings to be leased or sold. LBL
lands" (Concept Zero). Even a definition of recreation as it
applied to LBL was given by TVA in July of 1963. It stated,
"It will include 'only those activities that could be pursued by
tourists who wanted to visit a protected area. If people wanted
lodging, food, drink, or supplies, they would have to leave. . .
to buy what they wanted. They could then return to the
camping areas, but the managed environment would be
protected."

    Some of you may be asking now, "So what is the
problem? What is going on with the Land Between the Lakes
that would interest me or apply to me?" The answer is that a
great deal is happening that may endanger the future of this
beautiful peninsula that is so unique to the United States.

    In 1996, Tennessee Valley Authority publicly denied
the promises formerly made to landowners of the region. It
instead introduced a plan called Five Concepts. This plan
called for the construction of a resort hotel, golf course, theme
park, and land leases to private entrepreneurs. In 1997, work
began on a complex that is to include a tack store, bunkhouse,
restaurant, and grocery store. In addition to the proposed and
continued commercialization, logging on LBL is increasing at
startling rates (Concept Zero).

Student 10 (Continued)

references are incomplete, as is often the case with a rough draft. The student's list of works cited is still very much

> While some people, such as fellow classmate Tim Carter, agree that private industry "could help more people be exposed to the grandeur of LBL "the most common reaction I have encountered is similar to those of Mary White and Jonathan Adams: They feel that ". . .I don't want the private industry to use them [wilderness lands] for mining and stuff. We should preserve this wonderful national resource." Terry Brewer of Salt Lake City believes that although some people may lose their jobs, it is worth preserving the lands for the future (Hatch 44).
>
> In response to the public outcries TVA received, representatives belittled the promises made to the original landholders with the claim that they were informal, verbal, and "ancient history" (Concept Zero). It is even believed by some that if TVA fears removal of power over LBL by Congress, that it will "take action detrimental to the 170,000 acre tract," or at least do terrible harm with over-commercialization and mismanagement (Concept Zero).
>
> So, what is there to do? First of all, we must realize that it is up to us to stop the process of commercialization and destruction to the LBL region. Talk to senators, representatives, mayors, and whoever else with law-making ability. Realize that if LBL is allowed to be commercialized and logged, it not only leaves future generations a raw deal (that of having no wilderness land to enjoy), but it also tells TVA that it is okay for them to renege on the promises they made to landholders, essentially setting up a basis that provides for anyone to take land away and not have to honor their word to reimburse you.
>
> In my opinion, Tennessee Valley Authority is in the wrong. They gave their word to those people who had lived on

Student 10 (Continued)

at the rough draft stage, but it serves well enough to remind the student and any initial readers what the outside sources are.

---

the LBL land for generations, and it doesn't matter if it was verbal, written, formal, or informal — they made a promise. Honoring their promises is the least they can do for the families that lost their homes for the sake of public recreation.

Works Cited

Hatch—Do the Right Thing: Protect Earth (Terry Brewer)

Internet

Personal interview

Student 10 (Continued)

The instructor focuses quite a bit of attention on stylistic matters, but the longest recommendation suggests content revision encouraging the student to examine multiple sources and not become too dependent on one possibly biased source (and this point is stressed at the end).

Instructor's Comments to Student 10's Paper:
Overall, you've done a nice job. Your intro is particularly strong. Here are my recommendations:
1.   Throughout, work on combining small paragraphs into larger, meatier ones. As it exists, your writing more closely resembles journalism style (which is fine but which isn't always acceptable for academic writing across campus).
2.   See if you can't remove this and create a more interesting sentence with a strong verb.
3.   You might use some other identifier here...such as local university student or some other authority builder... especially since you don't actually identify yourself as a student until later in the paper.
4.   Don't bump quotes together from different speakers without a lead-in; it can confuse your readers.
5.   Of course, much of your material is coming from Concept Zero. Before you adopt their tone, keep in mind that their material may be biased and may have ulterior motives of its own. Do you ever actually hear TVA's response? In their defense, isn't it necessary to somehow pay for the beauty? How do they maintain minimal operating standards? (Higher user fees in lieu of commercialization?) No matter how little they build, there are still MANY people visiting each year. How does TVA pay to cope and educate all these people?
6.   Try an -ing phrase here and see if it's smoother.
7.   Should the government be plural here? (And should TVA? I used TVA in a plural sense above.. .just want to make you think about which pronoun actually is appropriate).
8.   This seems a bit informal.
Overall, work on paragraphing. Specifically on this paper, consider point 5 above.

Student 10 (Continued)

For the portfolio, this student included brightly designed tab pages for each assignment. The extra work makes the portfolio appear polished and indicates student pride. Such effort complements, but does not replace, strong writing.

Student 10 (Continued)

This student worked to reorganize paragraphs, expanding and combining them throughout the paper. The paper also includes corrected internal citations following

---

Revised Paper, Student 10:
Student 10
Professor G. Claywell
English 104-01
10 February 1999

Promises

When President John F. Kennedy included the Tennessee Valley Authority (TVA) in his vision of a "great nationwide land reclamation project" in 1963, his purpose was two-fold (Concept Zero, History of). His idea was to create a recreational area that would stay as close to "wilderness condition" as possible while attracting enough visitors to stimulate the regional economy with tourist capital (Concept Zero, What is). The area in Western Kentucky and Tennessee, originally referred to as "Between the Rivers," was to be made available for low-impact recreational activities, such as "fishing, hunting, hiking, camping, boating, and environmental education" (Concept Zero, History of).

One major problem existed, however, in the President's plan for what would later come to be known as "Land Between the Lakes" (LBL). This property happened to be owned by private citizens, many of whom had ties to the land dating as far back as the Revolutionary War, and they were not at all thrilled with the idea of selling (Concept Zero, History of). Yet something obviously caused the residents of the land to leave since LBL is now the 170,000 acre protected home of approximately 1300 plant species, 600 animal and bird species, and 76 species of fish (Concept Zero, What is). But what was it? Or, better yet, who was it?

Student 10 (Continued)

MLA format. The student "cleaned up" stylistic and
sentence-level concerns expressed by the instructor;

> When the families in the Kentucky/Tennessee region
> refused to move, Tennessee Valley Authority gave them no
> choice - they invoked "eminent domain" and practically stole
> the land from the remaining residents (Concept Zero, You
> Asked). But to smooth over the situation, TVA representatives
> made many verbal promises to the LBL refugees, keeping in
> line with the mission that Kennedy set out to achieve (Concept
> Zero, History of). Among these assurances were: "unimpeded
> access...to the numerous small cemeteries, no commercial
> development within the LBL lands, no occupied dwellings to
> remain or be built on LBL lands, and no private inholdings to
> be leased or sold on LBL lands" (Concept Zero, Summary).
> Even a definition of recreation as it applied to Land Between
> the Lakes was given by TVA in July of 1963. It stated, "It will
> include 'only those activities that could be pursued by tourists
> who wanted to visit a protected area. If people wanted
> lodging, food, drink, or supplies, they would have to leave...to
> buy what they wanted. They could then return to the camping
> areas, but the managed environment would be protected"
> (Concept Zero, History of).
>
> Some of you may be asking now, "So what is the
> problem? What is going on with the Land Between the Lakes
> that would interest me or apply to me?" The answer is that a
> great deal is happening that may endanger the future of this
> beautiful peninsula that is so unique to the United States.
>
> In 1996, Tennessee Valley Authority publicly denied
> the promises formerly made to landowners of the region. It
> instead introduced a plan called Five Concepts. This plan
> called for the construction of a resort hotel, golf course, theme
> park, and land leases to private entrepreneurs. In 1997, work
> began on a complex that is to include a tack store, bunkhouse,

Student 10 (Continued)

however, the student might have expanded some sections and might have included more outside sources, if they were available.

restaurant, and grocery store. In addition to the proposed and continued commercialization, logging in LBL is increasing at startling rates (Concept Zero, History of).

While some people, such as Murray State student Tim Carter, agree that private industry "could help more people to be exposed to the grandeur of LBL," the most common reaction I have encountered is similar to those of Mary White and Jonathan Adams. "...I don't want the private industry to use them [wilderness lands] for mining and stuff," Mary stated. Jonathan's reaction was similar to Mary's. "We should preserve this wonderful national resource," was Jonathan's reaction. Terry Brewer of Salt Lake City believes that although some people may lose their jobs, it is worth preserving the lands for the future (Brewer 44).

In response to the public outcries Tennessee Valley Authority received, representatives belittled the promises made to the original landholders with the claim that they were informal, verbal, and "ancient history." It is even believed by some that if TVA fears removal of power over LBL by Congress, that it will "take action detrimental to the 170,000 acre tract," or at least do terrible harm with over-commercialization and mismanagement (Concept Zero, History of).

So, what is there to do? First of all, we must realize that it is up to us to stop the snowballing process of commercialization and destruction to the LBL region. Some people, such as myself, have yet to experience the beauty and harmony found in the Land Between the Lakes region. Being from Illinois, I had hardly taken notice of the name LBL before coming to school at Murray State University. Now, I

Student 10 (Continued)

Notice that the student fails to include one source: the interview with fellow student Jonathan Adams.

feel as if visiting the area is a privilege I must take advantage of before something happens to alter the quiet wonder found there.

Talk to senators, representatives, mayors, and other officials with lawmaking ability. We must realize that if Land Between the Lakes is allowed to be commercialized and logged, it not only leaves future generations a raw deal (that of having no wilderness land to enjoy), but it also sends Tennessee Valley Authority the message that it is okay for them to renege on the promises they made to landholders, essentially setting up a basis allowing the government to break its promises with little or no consequence.

In my opinion, Tennessee Valley Authority is in the wrong. They gave their word to those people who had lived on the LBL lands for generations, regardless of whether the promise was verbal, written, formal, or informal - they made a promise. Honoring their promises is the least they can do for the families that lost their homes for the sake of public recreation.

Works Cited

Brewer, Terry. <u>Arguing in Communities</u>. Ed. Gary Layne
    Hatch. Mountain View: Mayfield, 1996.
Carter, Tim. Personal Interview. 29 January 1999.
Concept Zero. "History of the Land Between the Lakes."
    (27 January 1999):
    http://www.apex.net/lblcrisis/lblhistory.html
    (2 February 1999).
---. "Summary." (27 January 1999):
    http://www.apex.net/lblcrisis/bellwether.html
    (2 February 1999).

Student 10 (Continued)

---. "What is the Land Between the Lakes?"
(27 January 1999):
http://www.apex.net/lblcrisis/LBL.html
(2 February 1999).
---. "You Asked for It!" (27 January 1999):
http://www.apex.net/lblcrisis/docmentation.html
(2 February 1999).
White, Mary. Personal Interview. 29 January 1999.

Appendix G
Selected Portfolio Resources

Most of the information that exists on portfolios is actually addressed to the teachers who assign them (hence the need for this book!), but the following can give you additional insight and resources as you construct your portfolio.

Portfolio Resources Written for Students
Burch, Beth. *Writing for Your Portfolio.* New York: Allyn & Bacon, 999.

Electronic Portfolio Resources
Blair, Kristine L. and Pamela Takayoshi. "Reflections on Reading and Evaluating Electronic Portfolios." *Situating Portfolios: Four Perspectives.* Eds. Kathleen Blake Yancey and Irwin Weiser. Logan, UT: Utah State UP, 1997. 357-369.

Brewer, G. "FileMaker Pro [Computer Program]. Santa Clara, CA: Claris Corporation, 1994.

Grady, M. P. "Grady Profile [Computer Program]. St. Louis, MO: Aurbach & Associates, Inc., 1991.

Holmevik, Jan Rune and Cynthia Haynes. *MOONIVERSITY: A Student's Guide to Online Learning Environments.* New York: Allyn & Bacon, 2000.

Lankes, Anna Maria D. "Electronic Portfolios: A New Idea in Assessment." Syracuse, NY: ERIC Digest, 1995. ED 390377. 2/1/2000.
http://www.ed.gov/databases/ERIC_Digests/ed390377.html

Mt. Edgecumbe High School. "Digital Learner Portfolios." 2/1/2000.
http://www.mehs.educ.state.ak.us/portfolios/portfolio.html

Wagner, R. "HyperStudio" [Computer Program]. El Cajon, CA: Roger Wagner Publishing, Inc.

Portfolio Activities
"Ready-to-Use Portfolio Development Activities." Unit 6. *Writing Skills Curriculum Library*. Des Moines, IA: Center for Applied Research in Education, 1999.

Tully, Marianne. *Helping Students Revise Their Writing: Practical Strategies, Models, and Mini-Lesson that Motivate Students to Become Better Writers*. New York: Scholastic Professional Books, 1996.

Portfolios in Various Disciplines
Business
Lovitt, Carl R. and Art Young. "Portfolios in the Disciplines: Sharing Knowledge in the Contact Zone." *New Directions in Portfolio Assessment: Reflective Practice, Critical Theory, and Large-Scale Scoring*. Eds. Laurel Black, Donald Daiker, Jeffrey Sommers, and Gail Stygall. Portsmouth, NH: Boynton/Cook, 1994. 334-346.

Math
Mumme, Judy. "Portfolios: An Assessment Alternative." California Mathematics Project, Santa Barbara: Department of Mathematics, University of California, 1989.

Stenmark, Jean Kerr. "Assessment Alternatives in Mathematics: An Overview of Assessment Techniques That Promote Learning." Berkeley: University of California and California Mathematics Council *Campaign for Mathematics*, 1989.

Science
Beall, John. "Portfolios, Research, and Writing about Science" in *New Directions in Portfolio Assessment: Reflective Practice, Critical Theory, and Large-Scale Scoring*. Eds. Laurel Black, Donald Daiker, ,Jeffrey Sommers, and Gail Stygall. Portsmouth, NH: Boynton/Cook, 1994. 93-102.

Teacher Education

Campbell, Dorothy M., et al. *How to Develop a Professional Portfolio: A Manual for Teachers*. Boston: Allyn & Bacon, 1997.

Edgerton, Russell, Patricia Hutchings, and Kathleen Quinlan. *The Teaching Portfolio: Capturing the Scholarship in Teaching*. The AAHE Teaching Initiative of the American Association for Higher Education. 1991.

Yagelski, Robert P. "Portfolios as a Way to Encourage Reflective Practice Among Preservice English Teachers." *Situating Portfolios: Four Perspectives*. Eds. Kathleen Blake Yancey and Irwin Weiser. Logan, UT: Utah State UP, 1997. 225-243.

Portfolio Articles Explaining Teachers' Perspectives

Belanoff, Pat and Peter Elbow. "Using Portfolios to Increase Collaboration and Community in a Writing Program." *WPA: Writing Program Administration* 9 (1986):27-40.

Chiseri-Strater, Elizabeth. "College Sophomores Reopen the Closed Portfolio." *Portfolio Portraits*. Eds. Donald H. Graves and Bonnie S. Sunstein. Portsmouth, NH: Heinemann, 1992. 61-72.

Conway, Glenda. "Portfolio Cover Letters, Students' Self-Presentation, and Teachers' Ethics." *New Directions in Portfolio Assessment: Reflective Practice, Critical Theory, and Large-Scale Scoring*. Eds. Laurel Black, Donald Daiker, Jeffrey Sommers, and Gail Stygall. Portsmouth, NH: Boynton/Cook, 1994. 83-92.

D'Aoust, Catherine. "Portfolios: Process for Students and Teachers." *Portfolios in the Writing Classroom: An Introduction*. Ed. Kathleen Blake Yancey. Urbana, IL: NCTE, 1992. 39-48.

Graves, Donald. "Help Students Learn to Read Their Portfolios." *Portfolio Portraits*. Eds. Donald H. Graves and Bonnie S. Sunstein. Portsmouth, NH: Heinemann, 1992. 85-95.

Seger, F. Dan "Portfolio Definitions: Toward a Shared Notion." *Portfolio Portraits*. Eds. Donald H. Graves and Bonnie S. Sunstein. Portsmouth, NH: Heinemann, 1992. 114-124.

About the Author

    Dr. Gina Smith Claywell is an Assistant Professor at Murray State University who thinks that professors, like portfolios, should be personal. She is Director of Freshman Composition and loves teaching classes ranging from beginning composition to graduate courses in the teaching of composition. Her graduate coursework is from the University of Tennessee at Knoxville, and she formerly taught at East Central University in Ada, Oklahoma where she received the university's Teaching Excellence Award. She has essays in *Reforming College Composition: Writing the Wrongs* and *The Place of Grammar in Writing Instruction: Past, Present, Future* and articles/reviews in *Writing Lab Newsletter, Focuses,* and *Oklahoma English Journal.*

    At home, she is wife to Gerald, mom to Charlton and Catherine, co-caretaker of a menagerie of farm animals, harvester and chief preserver of garden produce, and, in short, often very tired but enjoying every minute of her hectic life. She sincerely hopes you find this book helpful as you compile your portfolio. You may contact her by email at gina.claywell@murraystate.edu or by phone at the Murray State University English Department at 270-762-2401.

Index